Safe at Home

Sports and Religion

A SERIES EDITED
BY JOSEPH L. PRICE

Books in the series:

Robert J. Higgs and Michael C. Braswell, *An Unholy Alliance: The Sacred and Modern Sports* (2004)

Allen E. Hye, *The Great God Baseball: Religion in Modern Baseball Fiction* (2004)

Marc A. Jolley, *Safe at Home: A Memoir on God, Baseball, and Family* (2005)

Joseph L. Price, ed., *From Season to Season: Sports as American Religion* (2001; 2004)

Forthcoming:

Eric Bain-Selbo, *Game Day and God: Football, Religion, and Politics in the South*

Craig Forney, *The Holy Trinity of American Sports*

W. David Hall, *Faith and Religion in the Big Blue Nation: The Cultural and Religious Sensibilities of the Kentucky Basketball Faithful*

Joseph L. Price, *Rounding the Bases: Essays on Baseball and Religion*

Safe at Home

A Memoir of God, Baseball, and Family

Marc A. Jolley

MERCER UNIVERSITY PRESS
MACON, GEORGIA

© 2005 Mercer University Press
1400 Coleman Avenue
Macon, Georgia 31207
All rights reserved

First Edition.
MUP/H666/P333

The paper used in this publication meets the minimum requirements
of American National Standard for Information Sciences—
Permanence of Paper for Printed Library Materials,
ANSI Z39.48-1992.

Library of Congress Cataloging-in-Publication Data

Jolley, Marc A.
Safe at home : a memoir of God, baseball, and family /
Marc A. Jolley.--
1st ed. p. cm.
Includes bibliographical references and index.
ISBN-10: 0-86554-740-8 (hardcover : alk. paper)
ISBN-10: 0-86554-909-5 (pbk. : alk. paper)
ISBN-13: 978-0-86554-740-7 (hardcover : alk. paper)
ISBN-13: 978-0-86554-909-8 (pbk.)
1. Jolley, Marc A. 2. Christian biography—United States.
3. Baseball—Religious aspects—Christianity. I. Title.
BR1725.J6435A3 2005
277.3'083'092—dc22
2005020708

For Susan, Patrick, and David;

for Mike and Tom;

for Mom;

and in memory of my Dad.

Listen to your life. See it for the fathomless mystery that it is. In the boredom and pain of it no less than in the excitement and gladness: touch, taste, smell, your way to the holy and hidden heart of it because in the last analysis all moments are key moments, and life itself is grace.

—Frederick Buechner, *Now and Then*

Contents

Preface	9
Acknowledgments	11
Foreword by Joseph Price	13
1. Play Ball	17
2. Waiting	27
3. Hope	39
4. Baseball Cards	47
5. Three Strikes, You're Out	55
6. God Went Down to Georgia	67
7. Baptism	75
8. Home Run	81
9. The Promised Land	89
10. Field of Dreams	117
11. Recreation	127
Appendix	131

Dad and me in 1959.

Preface

If doctors make bad patients, then do publishers and editors make bad writers? Perhaps, but the pull to write is too strong to resist. Flannery O'Connor tells us to write what we know. Ernest Hemingway said that he tried to write one true sentence at a time.

This book is what I "know." Each sentence is true. It is about me, and I "know" very little else. It is also about what I love: family, baseball, and God. But not necessarily in that order all of the time.

When my father died I decided that I needed to write something about myself so my sons would have an account of something about me that I felt was important. While this is not a full autobiography, it deals with three things in my life that have shaped it more than others. I have not written a lot about anyone. My brothers are rarely mentioned. But they have had and continue to have a profound impact on my life. Neither have I written about all the people who have changed my life for the better—or for the worse. And, I have said very little about my passion for books. That is another book.

Rather, I have written about how my faith, my love of family, and my love for baseball have all been connected. The place of this connection is home. My faith is included here because I am a believing Christian. My faith intentionally permeates nearly everything I do or think or say. Sometimes I think, do, and speak without intention, and that's when I do something I probably should not have done. My love of family comes above all, but my love of baseball has been constant along with church and family all the years of my life.

    For my life of faith I thank my mother who took me to church in the first weeks of my life. And for my love of baseball I thank my father who gave me a ball and glove not long after I started going to church. For my love of family I owe my parents for providing a loving home, and my two older brothers who were always there for me. And, I owe Susan, Patrick, and David, who make family the greatest experience in the world. Ever since I was born, these three—family, God, baseball—have not only been a part of my life, but have been the roots of my existence.

Note: I never sought publication for this book by Mercer University Press. I wrote and self-published (100 copies) an earlier—and much shorter—version for family and friends. I was encouraged by many to flesh it out and seek publication. Joseph Price, the editor of our sports and religion series was one of those. I told him that I could have no say in its publication at Mercer and so he contacted my supervisor Horace Fleming, executive vice president of Mercer University. They agreed that Mercer should do the book. And the staff of Mercer University Press has graciously agreed to endure this endeavor. Any royalties or profits go to the Press.

Acknowledgments

I want to thank…

—Edd Rowell for proofreading this book in its earliest edition. He is the best editor I know. He is an even better friend. He is in no way responsible, however, for any mistakes that are still in this book. I alone am liable.

—The Burts: the talent of Jim and Mary-Frances Burt is exceeded only by their encouraging spirit and endless friendship. Their design work is captivating.

—Marsha Luttrell who, when I told her that I had written this book, was genuinely supportive. She encouraged me to think of having this published by a real publisher, and for that faith I am forever grateful, even though I could not even make an attempt at someone rejecting "my" story.

—Joseph L. Price for wanting to publish this book in the series Sports and Religion. Joe's encouragement and pursuit are humbling. This book would not be published without Joe's help, and I owe him tickets to a game somewhere sometime.

—Horace Fleming, my supervisor and my friend, who when approached by Joe Price urging that Mercer University Press should publish a book by its own director agreed that it was a good idea. Horace is a gentleman and a scholar, in the truest sense of the words.

—Joan Godsey, Walter B. "Buddy" Shurden, Kay Shurden, Richard F. Wilson, and Nancy Stubbs, members of the Mercer community who not only read my advance copy but liked it and took time to tell me what they thought.

—Pam Durso of the Baptist Heritage & History Society and my pastor Jim Dant for their encouragement.

—R. Kirby Godsey, president of Mercer University, and the Press Board of Directors for the greatest support imaginable for a university press.

—The staff of Mercer University Press for their endurance in this endeavor. They enthusiastically agreed to pursue the publication of this book and for that I am eternally grateful. So Edd, Marsha, Kevin, Dana, Barbara, Amy, and Jenny, I thank you for backing a project such as this.

—Kevin Manus, who copyedited the text and who made many suggestions to improve the book. Kevin asked me to consider things and write things that no one else suggested. Thanks for pushing me in the right direction.

—Susan, my wife, for putting up with my love of baseball. She does because she knows that she and our sons are far more important than where the Yankees and Braves are in the standings.

—Patrick and David for being the reasons I wrote this book. They are God's greatest gifts.

Foreword

About a half century ago Robert Frost metaphorically trekked out of snowy wintry woods and into a summertime field of dreams. From there, he wrote in *Sports Illustrated*, "Some baseball is the fate of all of us." Frost, of course, was writing in a diamond era of baseball in America when Mickey Mantle, Willie Mays, and Duke Snider were gracing the outfields of New York ballparks; when Jackie Robinson, Larry Doby, and Don Newcombe were breaking down the color line in twentieth-century professional baseball; and when the young Hall of Famers Hank Aaron, Roberto Clemente, and Sandy Koufax were establishing new standards of excellence by players from various ethnic backgrounds.

During Frost's time a sense of innocence and genuineness typified players' celebrations of stellar plays and career accomplishments. Then, steroids had not yet tainted play and records, and players' statistics seemed pure, challenged only by questions of "what if…?" For example, what would the career totals of strikeouts or homeruns have been for baseball heroes (like Bob Feller and Ted Williams, who was Frost's favorite player) if they had not chosen to trade their baseball uniforms for battle gear for several mid-career years? Or how many Major League wins and RBIs might have been accumulated by African-American players (like Satchel Paige and Monte Irvin) if they had not spent most of their careers in the Negro Leagues? In the middle of

Frost's century, baseball helped to focus attention on these issues of patriotic service and social justice.

Certainly Frost sensed the social import and impact of baseball, but even more than its civic significance he perceived the strong sense in which baseball connects generations. In years since various authors have reflected specifically on their bonding with parents and children through baseball. In *Fathers Playing Catch with Sons*, Donald Hall poetically reflects on the special connections that baseball allowed him to develop with his father and his son. Even Hall's love of baseball itself is shaped by family baseball stories, both real ones (like his son's taunting tale of Donald's having dropped a homerun ball at Tiger Stadium) or ones perhaps imagined (like the one about his father having refused a Minor League contract in order to provide for his family). Thinking of these stories and these relationships, Hall sums up baseball and life in two sentences. "Baseball is fathers and sons playing catch, lazy and murderous, wild and controlled, the profound archaic song of birth, growth, age, and death. This diamond encloses what we are."

Although more eloquent than many essays, Hall's reminiscence is not unique. Throughout Ron Fimrite's *Birth of a Fan*, for instance, two full stanzas of award-winning authors present brief autobiographical reflections about their fascination with baseball and the meaning of life. Many of the stories, like those of Mark Harris and Anne Lamott, feature formative family journeys to ballparks, while others, like Robert Creamer's, debunk the romance of Hall's patriarchal title. Also moving beyond the masculine model of Hall's essay, Doris Kearns Goodwin verifies the possibility that baseball can establish distinct family and friendship ties for girls and mothers. In *Wait Till Next Year* she sympathetically remembers the close relationship that she developed with her father through their common devotion to the Dodgers, and she suffuses her account with reflections about how her Catholic faith and practice informed and challenged her love of baseball.

Now, in *Safe at Home*, Marc Jolley adds to this burgeoning genre of baseball memoir by reflecting theologically about the significance of the sport as it has shaped his worldview and daily practice—his affection for his father, his love of his sons, and his devotion to the Yankees. In one spiritually and filially poignant passage, Jolley reflects on the interconnections among salvation, baptism, and humility. The depth of the discussion with his father about these matters is marked by the uniqueness of Reggie Jackson's accomplishment in hitting three home runs on three pitches in Game 6 of the 1977 World Series. The counterpoint to their conversation is provided by Jackson's braggartly way: While Jolley's father modestly reveals the genuine character of his own salvation experience, Jackson's dramatic accomplishment brings victory—baseball's salvation—to the Yankees.

Enjoying baseball, fans feel at home, as they also will in reading about Jolley's personal experience of comfort, familiarity, and deep pleasure in baseball. This certain security and profound pleasure were noted also by Frost, who added a personal endorsement to his succinct observation about the social significance of baseball: "For my part," he confessed, "I am never more at home in America than at a baseball game."

In *Safe at Home*, thoughtful baseball fans will find moments that resonate with their own desires to wear an official uniform of Little League Baseball, to play whiffle-ball or backyard baseball with brothers and childhood friends, or simply to root with parents and children for one's favorite team. Jolley's personal testimony in *Safe at Home* makes a distinct contribution to the Mercer University Press series on *Sports and Religion*, for he manifests the spiritual power of confession while his love of baseball, God, and family shapes his faith and gives him voice.

Joseph L. Price
Editor, Sports and Religion Series

1

Play Ball!

> A ballplayer spends a good piece of his life gripping a baseball, and in the end it turns out that it was the other way around all the time.
> —Jim Bouton

> And on the eighth day, God said, "Play Ball!"
> Anonymous

I know I was alive before I was introduced to baseball, but I never really breathed until I started playing. The first glove I ever had was a piece of orange, flexible plastic that was shaped like a glove. It came with a ball and plastic bat. I don't remember playing with it very much. But I can still see it. I used to hold that glove and ball when I watched the game of the week with my dad. It was usually the Yankees against somebody. Dad would tell me stories of watching Mickey Mantle hit balls out of the park, how Yogi Berra could "knock 'em over the right field wall," and how nothing ever got past Clete Boyer at third.

I was too young to play when I saw my first games in the Little League. With two older brothers I had to sit through their games, and the whole time I wished I were playing. They played for the Yankees in the twelve-and-under league. Even in Cleveland, Tennessee, the Yankees ruled my world. In 1964 when I was five, there was no major league team in the South. In fact, other than a few teams in the American League, I knew of no one else. The Yankees and Mickey Mantle ruled the universe. My dad taught me that. I learned that there were other teams because my brothers' team played *other* teams. Just as there are two peoples in the world, Jews and Gentiles, there are two baseball teams: the Yankees and the other teams.

Having only to watch was difficult. Sure, I was able to play catch in the backyard with two big brothers, but after three years of waiting, this became more than I could bear. It was like learning to swim while standing on the shore. I knew the motions, knew all the rules, knew to swing level, and knew to keep my right foot planted when batting. But hitting "air home runs" was too easy. I wanted a challenge.

Finally, when I was seven, there was T-ball. The Yellow Jackets came drafting and I was ready. We had yellow and white jerseys and yellow hats. This was not the yellow of the Georgia Tech Yellow Jackets, which is more gold than yellow. No, it was the color of that crayon labeled "Yellow." No matter, I had my first jersey, and I am sure Mickey Mantle read about *me* in the paper.

I was the pitcher. A pitcher in T-Ball seems as useless as a floatation device on an airplane. But when you consider that when most kids try to hit the ball, they end up pummeling the tee, I fielded a lot of dribblers. Nonetheless, T-ball was the true beginning of my life. Whether it was battering the ball on the black plastic tee or catching a line drive, I knew then that my life had meaning. God made me a baseball player. Like Roberto Alomar said of himself, "I was sent here to play baseball." That's just the way I felt. More than that, it was just about the only thing my dad ever played with me.

Summertime in East Tennessee was humid. Playing catch with my brothers or my dad in the backyard was always eventful. We lived in a three-bedroom house with a small backyard. At one end of the backyard was a wooden fence. At the other, the edge of our yard was clearly delineated by what seemed to me at the time a forest of pine trees. It was about the size of the lot our house was on. At the end of the pine trees was the next house. The problem was that the pine trees were on a downward slope that was always covered in pine straw, a gardener's natural resource. When we would play catch with our backs to the trees, the ball would inevitably get past one of us and the ball would go all the way down into the neighbor's yard. This mishap would cause yelling and screaming and terrible accusations between my brothers and me. Each trip down the slope, one of us would risk the strong probability of slipping and falling, or worse, sliding face-forward right into one of the trees. Even though this trip down through the trees would happen many times during an afternoon, and even though we would scream at each other, there was not a chance we would stop playing. We would each hold the others hostage by saying that if the other threw the ball down there one more time, then we would quit. Yet, all the trips I ever took down that slope was worth a single afternoon of sweat and fun. To hold that cowhide-covered ball and to have the scent of that glove on my hand at bedtime from the day's game of catch was worth a hundred trips. I preferred sleeping with the scent of my sweat, the dirt from the ball, and the leather of the glove that had blended to a formula that rivaled ambrosia. My mother, of course, disagreed.

When I played catch with my dad, I never let his back be to the trees. He and I both insisted that he be close to the fence. If anyone was going to chase the ball down through the forest of pines, it would be me. It's not because if I missed the ball that I would have to go down there. He was always tired. Some days his accuracy was not reliable. His arm was used to his daily work at a plant I only knew the name of, DuPont. I had no idea then and no idea now what he did at work. All I know is he commuted the 60-mile round-trip for thirty-four years, worked overtime as much as he could to pay for vacations and Christmas, and that the job made him so tired that the only way to relax at night was to take a drink.

My backyard with the pine trees behind me in June 1968.

Something tormented dad—his job, his childhood, his time in the National Guard, perhaps something else—but the truth is that taking a drink was probably a habit that started so long ago that even he would not have been able to tell us how.

But those days he and I would play catch were magical. I could be Denny McLain going for win number 30; or Bob Gibson throwing a fastball while falling off of the mound towards first, or even Phil Niekro lofting a knuckler. We would be outside for thirty minutes or so and soon he would have to stop and smoke a cigarette. Sweat would trickle down from his temple, or bead up on his forehead. Soon he would put out the cigarette and say he needed to go in, that he was tired.

Sad is the only word I can use to describe my feelings. Dad's work was swing shift. That means he worked a week of day shift, a week of second shift, and a week of third shift, and then start over again. The problem was that his weeks were staggered and so he had only one weekend off each month. I could never understand his being tired. So time with him was precious. When he would quit throwing the ball with me it hurt. Sometimes it felt like he did not want to be with me.

I know that was never the case, but as a kid, it hurt when Dad said, "I'm done."

Sometimes I would stay outside and throw the ball in the air pretending to be Bobby Murcer running to catch a fly in centerfield. Sometimes the ball went on top of the house and rolled into the gutter. Most of the time I would simply go in, get my box of baseball cards, climb up on my bed, and read every one of them for the umpteenth time. I can still see the pictures on those cards. Hank Aaron holding his bat on his right shoulder, looking off to his left as if a pitcher were throwing the ball that would soon end up in the cheap seats. Clete Boyer holding his glove out in front of him like a vacuum cleaner. Harmon Killebrew having just swung the bat and watching the ball sail. Those cards were all I read. Reading books was for school. Fun reading meant reading the backs of these gifts from God, baseball cards. I learned math, division, fractions, percentages, and multiplication from those cards.

When summer arrived in 1967, my life changed again. Out of school meant not just the arrival of summer, but that baseball would finally begin. No more tees to hit off of, no more pretend pitcher. Honest to goodness Little League. I was eight years old and my dream was coming true. While the ages ranged from nine to twelve in our Little League, I would be the youngest on the team. Both of my brothers were on the same team. I had made the roster of the Yankees. I took it seriously. While too young, I must have been allowed on the team for family reasons.

I loved practice. Mom or dad would take all three of us to the school playground where we practiced two or three times a week. John Geitner, a USPS letter carrier, was our coach. He seemed ancient, but he was a good man. Dad liked him a lot. Mike, my oldest brother, pitched and played infield. Tom, my other brother, is a year younger than Mike but four years older than me, and he was a catcher, but played wherever he was needed.

I have a photograph on my bedroom wall from that year—all three of us on the same team. In those days, we used the same hand-me-down uniforms year after year. At the end of the season, you gave it back to the coach and he kept them all until the next season. Some players had a "Y" on the left breast of their jersey. Some had "Yankees" written across the front. The word "Yankees" is barely visible on my uniform. I am squinting with the sun in my face. Holding my glove on my knee as if I have my whole career ahead of me.

Near the end of my first season, we were playing the Senators. We had a few guys on vacation and were a little short on players. That night we had ten. I would not play until the end of the game, but I knew I would play some. The coach always let everyone play. We were losing 8-0 and we had yet to get a hit. In the fifth inning (our games were only six innings long), I was put in to play right field. In the bottom of the fifth, I came to bat. With encouragement from parents, coach, and teammates, I stood there as an eight-year-old against one of the two best pitchers in the league.

He pitched and I swung. And in one of those few moments of completeness in the universe when the stars were properly aligned and God shined his grace my way, my bat connected and I hit a linedrive to left center. I was so surprised, that I almost forgot to run. There was a collective gasp in the crowd (I thought of thousands) of twenty-five or so parents and siblings. I had broken up the no-hitter. The ball nearly went to the fence on a couple of bounces but I dared not run past first. I was scared to death. We lost 9-0.

The next day, my dad came in with the newspaper after work. The normal procedure at supper time was that when dad arrived (when he was working the day-shift) around 4:50 P.M. he would open the door, walk in through the kitchen, say "Hey" to whoever was there, walk back to his bedroom, go to the bathroom, wash his hands, and in about ten minutes reemerge and sit at the table where supper would be waiting, promptly at 5:00 P.M. We would eat some kind of meat, mashed potatoes, a vegetable that none of us liked except mom and/or dad, and some kind of bread. Whatever we were having, there would always be bread: cornbread, canned biscuits, or brown-'n-serve rolls. The adage "man shall not live by bread alone" was not allowed in our house. In fact, the one time I quoted this biblical wisdom, my dad looked at me and said, "Yes, I can!"

But on this evening, dad came in with the paper and called me into the living room. Though the *Cleveland Daily Banner* was a daily paper, it was small on weekdays, except for Wednesdays when it swelled with all the grocery ads. He turned quickly to the sports page. Half the sports page covered major league baseball. One-fourth covered other insignificant events. One-fourth covered the Little League games. He read quickly, took his pen from his pocket, and underlined my name. The sentence read that the pitcher "had a no-hitter in the fifth until Mark [sic] Jolley singled." I was a star. Name misspelled and all, I was a star.

I wondered if Mickey Mantle had seen the paper.

2

Waiting

> You look forward to it like a birthday party when you're a kid. You think something wonderful is going to happen.
> —Joe DiMaggio, on Opening Day

> But those who wait for the Lord
> shall renew their strength,
> they shall mount up with wings like eagles,
> they shall run, and not be weary,
> they shall walk and not faint.
> —Isaiah 40:31

All spring long I used to wait for baseball. We would start our season long after the big leaguers were playing. And there was nothing more special than opening day. I guess that could be true in a lot of sports.

But while I played midget football and later basketball, there was nothing comparable to the opening day of baseball season.

School was always in the way. Except that it was at school that I shared my dreams with my friends. Usually, in the spring, my dreams and the dreams of my friends were centered on baseball and Little League. Waiting for opening day was as painful than waiting for Christmas.

When I waited for Christmas, the thing I always wanted but I never got was a box of baseball cards. There were two reasons for this. When I was a kid, you could not buy an entire box from a dealer or a shop or on the Internet like you can now. The only way to buy them would be to go to the store and buy a box at full price *if* you could find a box unopened. But the main reason was that they were simply not available before Christmas. So, I sometimes got a football, or a Packers sweatshirt or a Dolphins jacket. Those were great Christmas gifts, but there was nothing baseball related. Now, you can order sports memorabilia anytime of the year.

Still, waiting for Christmas was an arduous task. It required patience and perseverance. I had little patience, and I persevered only because human nature would not allow me to quit. But waiting for opening day in baseball was gut wrenching. The only thing that helped was that we would start to practice a couple of weeks before the season began. We would usually meet at a school nearby around 5 or 5:30 and practice for about an hour or so. I can't remember if we practiced every day or not, but I know that however much we practiced, it wasn't enough. I could have played all day. I often wondered how great life would be if we practiced from 8:00 to 3:00 P.M. and had school from 5:00 to 6:00 P.M.

Finally, after much gnashing of teeth, the morning would come. In Cleveland, Tennessee, opening day was a very special day in the community. It was not just a matter of arriving at the ballpark and playing. It meant that we would have a parade.

Our Little League had four divisions (There was no interplay until the all-star season began after the regular season.). Each team and every player would meet in full dress complete with glove—and sometimes catchers wore their masks—at the parking lot of the Village shopping center (there were no such things as malls, yet). We would pile into cars and trucks and lineup and make the trek from the shopping center parking lot up Keith Street all the way to the ballpark.

We would scream and shout and brag and roar in all our glory about how great we were. All traffic stopped and people blew their horns and shouted with us and for us. At that one moment in time, we were all tied for first place and none of us had struck out and none of us had cried on the field and none of us had made an error. It was nearly perfect. The excitement was such that you would have thought that we were on our way to heaven. And for boys like us, we were.

Upon arriving at the ballpark, we excitedly jumped out of the cars, trucks, and whatever else may have brought us. We would line up and march into the field where we would stand, waiting. Someone always had to say something. And then someone else would say something, and on and on. But eventually, we came to that moment that does not happen anymore: the convocation. A public prayer. When I was in Little League I knew nothing of religious differences. To me, everyone believed in God and Jesus. So, the prayer was natural before the first pitch.

In Cleveland, Tennessee, there was school, sports, and church, but not in that order. There were lots of Baptists and Methodists. There was one Catholic Church. They were always looked on with suspicion. I had no idea what "catholic" meant until one of my best friends, David Froula, told me he was Catholic, and so I went to church with him once.

But what we were known for in Cleveland, Tennessee, was for the Church of God. Now, there is more than one kind of Church of God but when you're a kid, there's just one. The point is, however, that Cleveland was a very religious town. Everyone, it seemed, went to church somewhere, although it was clearly obvious that not everyone was Christian.

So the prayer was said and it seemed to drag on

longer than waiting for Christmas. The guy would pray for this team and that cause and for the weather and for sportsmanship and for good attitudes and for everything in the world like our troops in Viet Nam and for our president.... They would have a public prayer at events in Cleveland long after the crusade of Madalyn Murray O'Hair.

At the conclusion of the prayer, the national anthem was played on a record player, but one year we had a marching band perform it. There is no sound like 400 people, adults and kids, singing the national anthem at a Little League opening day.

Then, the person in charge would give the ceremonial charge, "Play Ball!" The wait was almost over. Some years we played on opening day, but in others we had to wait two days or more to play. But when we played on opening day it was the best.

Of course, being the home team was the best advantage in having last bat; I never liked being home team. It meant that there was a possibility that you would not get the last at bat if you were ahead. I hated missing a turn at bat. I had waited nine months to stand in the batter's box and I wanted every swing I could get. There was nothing better in life than standing waiting for the pitcher to hurl a ball that I had the chance of hitting. So, on opening day, I loved being the visiting team and batting first.

When I was between seven and ten I usually batted eighth or ninth, and that was the pits because

I might only get two at bats in a six-inning game, but usually I would get three. Later, I would bat either second or third and sometimes would get four at bats if we managed to score some runs.

Waiting. Waiting to bat on opening day was what we lived for. It defined us and gave us purpose. When I was nine, our Yankees team had high hopes that year. We had never been very good, but this year we thought we had a chance to win some games. I was due up eighth. When I stepped into the batter's box, there were two outs. I walked up, put dirt on my hands, adjusted my helmet, dug in and looked the pitcher right in the eye. Six pitches later, the wait was over and I had struck out. This was like having your proverbial bubble busted. It was not the way I wanted the season to begin, but I believed there was always another chance to hit. When the best hitters make outs two out of three at bats, you understand that one out is not a career. After all, Mickey Mantle struck out three times more than his total number of homeruns.

And that is the way the season went. We won only two games that year. But still today, after thirty-six years that at-bat stands out. Why?

Waiting. That spring and summer I was waiting for Jesus to return to earth. My family attended Stuart Park Baptist Church. It was a mission church of the First Baptist Church of Cleveland. Stuart Park was a small church with around 100 people on a good Sunday morning. My Sunday school teacher was Mr. Gault. He was a wonderful man who gave his time to teach boys my age. He was pleasant, considerate, and caring. I don't remember anything he ever said, but I remember the kind of person he was.

But Sunday school was safe. It was the sermons in worship that were problematic. We had a variety of preachers while I was there. Most of them were typical Old South, small-town preachers that were too afraid to tackle real problems in our world like opposing the Viet Nam war or fighting racism. Most addressed issues like rock 'n' roll and drugs and sex and, their very favorite, the end of the world.

Why intellectually challenged preachers believe they have to warn people about the end of the world is beyond me. They talk about it as if they know when the game is over and when everyone is least expecting it that God is going to lower the boom on us all. When our preachers were not preaching on this, our evangelists were. We would have revivals at least two times a year. But it seems like they all were about the same thing: the end of the world.

"If Jesus came back tonight, at the sound of the trumpet, right out of the sky and into your bedroom window, would you be ready to meet him?" they would ask. They would ask this over and over. It scared me to death.

This particular summer, when Tommy (my

brother and the middle brother at that) was thirteen, we were in the middle of a revival and the evangelist and our pastor came calling on Tommy. Now, Mike, our oldest brother, had already been saved and was going to heaven as sure as Mickey Mantle was headed for the hall of fame. But Tommy had yet to make that public decision by "walking down the aisle to accept Jesus Christ as Lord and Savior."

The evangelist and the pastor came into our house on Saturday afternoon to make sure that Tommy was going to be saved. They told him one thing after another. I stood outside our living room listening. I don't recall a single thing they said, but I remember being scared to death. Tommy accepted Christ right there on the spot. It was an offer he couldn't refuse.

After they left, I waited. I waited until bedtime. I slept some that night due to exhaustion. I wanted to be awake if Jesus came through my window so I could repent immediately and not go to hell. The next morning, the evangelist gave his rhetorical gem on the second coming regarding how we are going to hell if we were not Christian. I waited forever. It seemed that the sermon took an hour or more. It may have, in fact.

I waited. After he concluded his sermon, I waited through a prayer that would make the guy at the baseball park embarrassed. Finally, the wait was over. We began to sing the invitation. The invitation is that one chance we have to make all things right with God. Tommy went down front immediately. There were people crying for him, my mom especially.

What she did not notice was that I, too, was crying. I knew I had to walk that aisle and be saved. I did not want to burn in hell forever. I was scared to death. At the end of the first verse, I was sobbing and asked my mom to go with me. She did. She was sobbing, too.

The preacher asked me if I wanted Jesus Christ to live in my heart as my Lord and Savior, and I said yes. He asked me if I repented of all my sins, and I said yes. He told me that I was now God's child and that I was "saved by the blood of the lamb." I kept crying.

After the service, it seems that about 1,000 people—although it was not more than 100—came by and squeezed me and hugged me and kissed me. It went on forever. I went home exhausted. The wait was over. I was saved.

That night we went back for the final night of the revival. It sounded like the same sermon I had heard all week long. "If Jesus came back tonight, would you go to heaven or hell." I believed I would go to heaven, and that was comfort at last. The next Sunday, Tommy and I were baptized by our grandfather, Thomas Roscoe Jolley, a man who served Baptist churches in McMinn County, Tennessee, for more than fifty years preaching and screaming about the end of the world.

After mom said goodnight that night, I laid there in the dark. For months I had gone to bed on Sunday night thinking about that critical question: What if Jesus came back tonight. For months I was scared. That night, the night that should have been so wonderful, there was something wrong. Something terrible occurred to me. What if Jesus did come back tonight? I would never play baseball again. Now, that would be hell, I thought.

My prayers shifted from hoping I would go to heaven to hoping these preachers were wrong, that Jesus was not coming back soon. If he came back soon, I would miss my baseball life on this earth. What would be so great about that?

I had fears like this for years until we moved our church membership to Westwood Baptist Church where living the Christian life supplanted the scare tactics. By then, my baseball life as a player was over. But one thing is for sure: if they play baseball in heaven, I would wait an eternity for one more at bat.

Waiting is mostly a waste of time. So it seems, but there is grace in waiting. Each moment is important. Each moment is all we have. It may be spent waiting for the convocation to end. It may be spent looking out the window hoping for spring. It may be spent waiting for the pitcher to throw the first ball. It might be the moment you talked to a stranger or when you didn't. Or, it could be a moment that changes your life, like when I decided I would stop just looking at the young lady in the Hallmark Card shop and go in and introduce myself to my—unbeknownst to me—future wife. The here and now is all we are assured of, and God's promise of presence with us in that moment is all we have. But a moment should never be spent in fear that God may burst through a bedroom window. Those moments seem wasted, but their value is measured in how one responds to them. I have had plenty of such moments.

I no longer worry about Jesus appearing in my bedroom window, but I still have dreams that I am waiting for opening day. And those moments of hope and anticipation are some of the most exhilarating moments a person can have. But opening day in baseball is not all there is. I have two sons, born nine years and three days apart. Their birthdays are March 28 and March 31. Only baseball fans recognize the significance of the last week of March: it is the prelude to the beginning of the baseball season. Personally, opening day in major league baseball now signals the annual growth of my sons. I still look forward to opening day and celebrate it by watching *Field of Dreams* (see chapter 10 below) and whoever is playing that day. But each opening day represents another year in my sons' lives and Susan's and mine. Now, when I look out the window at night I think of something from a very different movie. In the movie

Finding Neverland, about the writing and staging of *Peter Pan*, James Barrie says, "Boys should never be made to go to bed. They always wake up a day older." Now every night I don't fear the coming of Jesus. Instead, I realize my sons are one day older and so are Susan and I. And as I lay there I wonder if the three of them have a clue about how deeply I cherished our moments together that day.

3

Hope

I never had it made.
—Jackie Robinson

Be Doers of the Word... Religion that is pure and undefiled... is this: to care for orphans and widows in their distress and to keep oneself unstained by the world.
—James 1

Timothy was his name. He was nearly a foot shorter than me. He was the smallest kid on our team. Since we usually lost, nobody really thought his size was a hindrance to our being champions. He didn't play that much. But like everyone in the league, he was supposed to play at least one inning in every game. That was a rule, and John Geitner, our coach, made sure everyone played in every game. Coach Geitner died on January 20, 2005. He had served his country in the army during World War II, and as a postal carrier for more years than people could remember. More importantly, he coached Little League baseball for more than thirty-six years.

Coach Geitner made sure Timothy played. Timothy was not very good, but he tried. It seems like he never missed a practice and never missed a game. While I still remember many of my teammates like Ashley Ownby, Tommy Walker, Jeff Ballenger, Lynn Chestnutt, Wes Snyder, and many other faces, Timothy was the most challenged guy I played with. I learned a lot from him.

In the late innings when Timothy would be in the field, we all secretly hoped against hope that if the ball were hit to him that he would catch it. Usually, there was not much of a chance of his making a catch if it had been a fly ball. He always misjudged flies, but one thing is for sure: he tried. Once he was hit in the chin when the ball nearly went in his glove. The other team laughed as their hitter rounded the bases, but our second baseman simply ran out and retrieved the ball and threw it in. Asked if he was okay, with a tear in his eye he said, "Yeah. Let'em try that again." He never gave up.

Sometimes I would find him after practice or after a game and I could tell he had been crying. One game after I had played catcher—I thought I was Joe

Torre—Timothy asked me if I thought he could be a catcher. "I don't know," I told him honestly, "it gets pretty dirty and scary back there sometimes. The outfield is much safer."

"No place is safe for me. I just thought if I had all those pads on that I might have a chance to live a longer life," he replied with a sense of humor.

Nonetheless, Timothy gave his heart to the game. When he batted, you could see intensity on his face no matter the pitch count. With every pitcher's wind-up you could see on Timothy's face that he had all the hope in the world. When he was in the outfield and the ball was hit, you would not see fear or nervousness on his face—it was always hope. He simply had no talent for playing baseball. I would have thought he was the most miserable feeling baseball player who ever lived.

My mom would often take me to town on Saturday morning for one or fifty errands. Cleveland was a smaller town when I was young. There were no malls or fast-food restaurants. Downtown we had the typical courthouse, post office, JC Penney, Woolworth's, and other such places. We had a great hamburger joint called the Spot. It had about ten stools for sitting, but they served great hamburgers and milkshakes. One particular Saturday morning, mom needed to go to the post office. She dragged me along. What I saw would change me. We drove downtown and circled the block for a parking place. We got out and began the ascent up the concrete steps.

Reclining on the steps was a man. Although, he looked more like he had just fallen on the steps and did not have the strength to reposition himself. His hair was matted down on one side, and yet stood in every direction on the other. He had not shaved in days, or weeks. Perhaps he had never shaved. His eyes were dark and nearly crossed. When he looked in a given direction, it appeared that only one eye moved. His mouth was grotesque. I am not sure if it was his teeth that resembled a bent rake or if it was a birth defect or if everything was distorted by the drool that proceeded from it.

His clothes were so tattered that they would have been rejected by any second-hand store. His brown coat surprised me since it was warm weather. The coat looked as if it had been melted on top of his button-down shirt, and both were beyond filthy. His pants were ragged and hung on his legs as though he were a scarecrow that had been disemboweled. In one hand he held a shoebox. In the other he held a cup of pencils. His hands shook. The pencils rattled as if they wanted to jump out of the cup.

He looked at me and stretched out his arm, the cup of pencils was shaking. As we began to climb the stairs, I thought the nice thing to do was to take one of the pencils he was offering. My mother quickly let me know that I should not go near him.

"Who is that?" I asked.

"Shhhh" was the reply.

We went in the post office and Mom took care of her errand and we left. He was still there. We walked down the opposite side of the steps, even though it was on the left side. At the foot of the steps, a man walked over and gave the strange man a dollar bill, then graciously took a pencil. The man on the steps uttered something in two syllables that had to be a "thank you." The upright man politely said, "You're welcome." The reclining man smiled.

When we got in the car, I repeated, "Who is that man?"

"Well, what can I tell you?" she said. She gave me his name. "He's had a hard life. He lives with his daddy. They are very poor."

"Why could I not get one of his pencils? He held them out to me."

"He wasn't giving them away. He was begging. You see, you give him some money and he will give you a pencil. That's the only job he can get."

"Why is he begging?" I asked.

"Because, his father is a no-good..." and she stopped. "The way I hear it is that his father sends him over here to beg all day long. When he gets home, his daddy beats him if he does not bring enough money home."

"Like daddy beats us with a belt when we've done something really bad?" I inquired sympathetically.

"No, not like that. When your daddy whips you, you deserve it. This poor man doesn't deserve to be treated that way." She continued, "His daddy is a drunk. He doesn't work and he lives off whatever he can find or steal. He takes every penny his son brings home. Then he drinks it all away and his son is left to make it on his own."

"He doesn't look like he eats very well. He—"

She interrupted me by changing the subject.

I saw him plenty more times in my life. But when I was not yet old enough to drive, it dawned on me that I had not seen him in a long time. I often wondered what happened to him. How he lived. How he died. Did his father kill him? Did he die and no one know about it? Was there a funeral?

After that year of baseball, I never saw Timothy again. I often think of both Timothy in the outfield and that man on the courthouse steps. Timothy was too small to make it in this world where size matters too much on the outside and not enough on the inside. They each had clothes hanging off them. Each looked as if the world had never noticed them for who they were. Sometimes I still see them transposed, each with arm outstretched, holding a cup or a glove, hoping against hope to make a catch.

Many years later, I would be in the library at seminary and read Luke 16. The rich man and Lazarus story changed my theology. Every time I think of

Lazarus to this day, I think he must have sat outside that gate selling pencils. Covered in sores, dressed in rags, too small to notice, and reaching out, he hoped against hope that he would catch someone's attention.

In his novel *Brendan*, Frederick Buechner wrote something that I copied and taped inside my Bible: "'To lend a hand when we're falling,' Brendan said, 'Perhaps that's the only work that matters in the end.'"

In the moment, the man at the courthouse caught my attention. I had done nothing.

4

Baseball Cards

> On the field, blacks have been able to be super giants. But, once our playing days are over, this is the end of it and we go back to the back of the bus again.
> —Hank Aaron

> And who is my neighbor?
> —Luke 10:29

Baseball cards were my best friends in the summer. Sure I played with other kids and had other friends. I played baseball on a team. I went to church. I had brothers. I even had neighbors. But when it came to being understood, only my cards knew the real me. Only those cards knew my dreams, my feelings, and my fears, because I talked to them.

They talked to me, too. I learned much from

baseball cards. I learned that Bobby Murcer not only married his high school sweetheart, but that he served in the armed services for two years. What more could you want from your hero than to know he married for love and friendship and that he served his country? He served me by playing for the Yankees. I also learned that Murcer was only the third Yankee in franchise history to earn $100,000 a year or more. Today, a player might lose that much in a week if he were suspended. But baseball cards introduced me to another issue. Race.

One Saturday in March 1968, my mom needed to go to S. S. Kresge's to do some shopping. Kresge's is a sister to the K-Mart stores. Our Kresge's was a huge store (or so I thought at the time). It was a place that had everything: clothes, snacks, dry goods, toys, underwear, lawn and garden supplies, you name it. It even had a snack bar where you could get hamburgers, hot dogs, sandwiches, and delicious hand-dipped ice-cream milkshakes and malts. As great as those malts were, my favorite place was the candy island. It was a long counter that outlined a rectangle, the middle open so employees could walk and help you on every side.

On this Saturday, when baseball would be starting soon, the thrill of thrills was to see if the first baseball cards had arrived. I had 40 cents and that would buy some packs of cards if they were available. I was so nervous that I thought I would be wet with sweat by the time I arrived at Kresge's. But we finally arrived and I was still dry. We got out of the car. I began to run across the way when my mom told me to wait for her and not to run out in front of a car. She was always a mother.

Opening the door, I took off in the direction of the candy island. Mom said that she would find me when she was ready. Those were the days when a kid could wander in a store and the parent did not worry about perverts snatching their kids. It was a time when if you acted up that any adult near you could give you verbal instruction and admonition to the delight of your parent. Not only that, it was expected.

Knowing the store almost as well as I knew my own house; I turned each corner at top speed. Rounding to the right by the table with the blue jeans and making a sharp left turn to the candy island, some employee (a new one, obviously) had erected a tower of jarred pickles. While I was a baseball player—immortalized now by the newspaper—my turning skills were not that good on a slick floor. I tried to deflate my body and twist it enough to miss the display, and nearly did. I apparently left my elbow out a bit too far and clipped one jar, and it was sent into the air. It looked like one of the ships on Star Trek that was hurling through space, end over end, slowly yet terminal. The pickles and shards of glass were all over the floor.

"You dumb a--!" the teenage employee yelled. He had a box in his hands.

"I'm sorry." I could see my baseball card money disappearing and I could feel my (dumb) butt burning from the belt I would get at home.

"I told you not to put those jars in the aisle like that. See what happens when you don't listen," came a voice from a woman who was apparently the teenager's boss.

It was like a miracle. One moment I was in mortal danger and the next this divine being had sided with me. She made him apologize to me. I was so stunned I mumbled, "That's okay," and ran down to the end of the aisle.

I searched the candy thoroughly to see if the cards were for sale yet. The excitement was nerve racking. There is only so much a nine-year-old can handle. Looking back on it now, I was nervous. It's that nervousness you get when the dentist doesn't find any cavities and you get to leave and go buy your favorite food as a reward. Or you do have cavities and not only do you not get your favorite snack, but you have to listen to mom complain the whole way home about health and money. You also get to dread the return trip facing a needle, a drill, and the hands of a smelly man in your mouth (They didn't use gloves then.). I should never have been taken to a dentist whose teeth were worse than mine, but that is another story.

Finally, eureka! There they were. One box of the best sight a nine-year-old boy could ever see. Only two packs were missing. I picked up four packs of cards. At 10 cents each, I only needed 2 cents from mom for tax. I might have to do an extra chore, but I would have painted the house for those 2 cents.

When I found her she quickly handed me the two cents.

"So, are you ready to go?" I asked.

"Not yet. Hold your horses!" She would always say that when I was in a hurry.

It seemed like hours but we finally made our way to the checkout counter. Running back outside with the same caution screamed at me, I made it to the unlocked car (Why would anyone ever lock their car in those days?) and jumped in the back seat. I had to push the seat belt out of the way. I remember thinking, "Why did they make those things, anyway?"

Each summer it would be the same dream: If I could get a Mickey Mantle card all would be well. I could die a happy boy. That day I opened four packs of baseball cards and I did not get a Mickey Mantle, but what I did get was just as good.

The four cards I remember were Hank Aaron, Willie Mays, Mel Stottlemyer, and Horace Clarke. Since Stottlemyer was a Yankee pitcher, and my favorite pitcher at that, I first thought his was the best card I got that day. Clarke was a scrappy second baseman for the Yankees, so that was a good card, too.

Aaron played for the Braves, and I had heard a lot about him and dared to like him. I knew of Mays because my grandfather thought he was the best in baseball, even though his son, my dad, thought Mantle was. Nonetheless, I began to digest the statistics on the back of Aaron and Mays. Those numbers told me of their greatness. Without ESPN to show ten games a week, all I had were cards and the newspaper to hear about those guys. Those two cards had few words, but as they say, a number is worth a thousand words.

I began looking at the other cards when my mom slowed the car and said, "Look, there is Mr. Jones. (I have long forgotten the man's name, but I will never forget his face.) I bet he needs a ride."

Mr. Jones was a large, late-middle-aged African American, although that term had not been dreamed of yet. Mom rolled down the window. "Hello there, Mr. Jones. Would you like a ride home?"

"Hello, Mrs. Jolley. I sure would," he responded in surprise.

He walked around to the other side and climbed in the front passenger seat. He had on some kind of aftershave lotion that was wearing thin, but still distinctive.

They exchanged small talk. After a few minutes we pulled up to the front of a house where he got out and gave my mom a big smile and thank you.

As we drove away I asked who he was. My mom

responded that she knew him from a previous job of hers. She concluded our conversation with an instruction: "Don't you ever tell your dad what we did by giving that man a ride. Do you understand?" When I asked why, she made a cryptic remark about him being black and that my dad would not understand. My dad knew the times. He would have helped the man, too, but would never have wanted my mom to help him.

I had never seen color until that day. I had seen black people, sure, but the color never struck me. That's just the way God made them. "Red and yellow, black and white..." the hymn went. What did mom mean? I knew one thing: I would never tell dad, and I've never told anyone until now.

Later that night I asked my mom about black people and she said that there is no difference between white people and black people except their color. Thirty-five years later I know that on that day my mom did a foolish thing. For a white woman to be seen with a black man in that day and time was dangerous for both, no matter what the reason. This is what my dad understood. But to my mom, this was a man she knew and worked with. She looked through the eyes of Christian charity, not the lenses of social and racial bias. She acted on faith. That single act has always been the Good Samaritan story for me. (The truth be told, my dad was not much different. He was known to stop and help people on the highway even as he grew older; he always lent a hand.)

I went to my room later and got ready for bed. My brother Tom shared the room with me and he was getting ready, too. Oblivious to the day's events, he soon told me to turn out the light as I was flipping through my baseball cards. After a couple of minutes he asked why I had not. I told him I was looking at my baseball cards one last time. I had just gotten them that day and wanted to look at them one more time.

"Hurry," he said.

"Just a minute," I responded. I paused on Hank Aaron, Willie Mays, and Horace Clarke. I noticed for the first time the differences in color. I thought about it for a while. I could still smell Mr. Jones's aftershave from the ride earlier. I got up and turned off the light, climbed back in bed, still holding my cards. Hank Aaron and Willie Mays were on top. I slid their cards off, put the others on the floor, and placed the Aaron and Mays cards under my pillow.

From that day forward, my monotheism of Mantle turned into a trinity. If mom treated black people as equals, then they were. If Mr. Jones could ride in my car, then Aaron and Mays had a place in my life. Hank and Willie, welcome to the table.

5

Three Strikes, You're Out

> I'd walk through hell in a gasoline
> suit to keep playing baseball.
> —Pete Rose
>
> Nice guys finish last.
> —Leo Durocher
>
> What then should we do?
> —Luke 3:10

Pitching for the Yankees in Little League was eventful in unusual ways. It was never a question of winning, because we almost never did. In fact, we would usually win maybe one or two games each year, and the thing you did not want to be in Cleveland, Tennessee, was the team that lost to the Yankees. What was eventful about pitching for the Yankees was comprised of two things: how much we would lose by and how we would lose. Our losses were an experience, whether by the unbelievable errors or losing 14–2. There was a 10-run rule: if you trailed by ten or more runs at the end of the fourth inning then the game was declared completed. We lost several by this rule.

The year I was eleven, we won only two games. Our first win (we were 2-13 for the year) came after we had lost the first seven or eight games. The way we would scream and hug after winning had to be embarrassing to the other team, to their parents, to our parents, and to our coach. But for that one moment we were thrilled beyond belief.

Little League taught me how to lose. Knowing how to lose is the best teacher for how to win. Nothing can ready you to be a winner like losing can. And we were good at losing. We would walk across the field with heads up and hearts heavy and shake the hands of those who had just annihilated us. We would then return to the dugout where our coach would say, "All right, the cokes are on me." Suddenly, we were almost happy and we would run around behind the stands and made our way to the concession stand for our reward for losing.

And this remained the same from ages nine to eleven. We would win one or two games a year, keep our heads up, and get our free cokes. When I was eleven I made the City All-Stars, not the more prestigious State All-Stars. This was a personal accomplishment but our team was still really bad. Our all-star team lost two in a row and suddenly we were out of the all-star tournament. I don't think anyone thought I was the reason. I played only one inning in each game. Still, I felt a little like Jonah. Had they thrown me over the dugout fence before the first game then perhaps they could have sailed on to victory.

But the next year was the most unusual of all. We began to win. That summer we went 11-4 and came in second place. I had my best year and pitched to a 5-0 record and hit nearly .700, but 0 home runs. Yes, I kept my own stats. I could tell you after every at bat my average, how many doubles and strikeouts I had. I played first and even caught some.

Winning after losing for so long was a humbling thing. We never tired of winning, but we never over celebrated. We knew something about how the other team felt. I learned some hard lessons that summer. One of the reasons we were improved that year was the arrival of a ten-year-old whiz "kid." He was a southpaw, he could hit, and his dad was Coach Geitner's new assistant coach.

I was by far the biggest guy on our team. I had grown over the winter and I knew this would be my best year ever. In fact (or fantasy), I could see my hits sailing over the fence and me trotting around the bases like Hank Aaron.

But the new kid's dad had other ideas. He may have seen me as a threat to his son's glory. So, in a move that confused both my dad and me, the kid's father asked me to hit second in the lineup. In doing so, he told me to stop swinging for the fences, and just make contact.

I took orders well. I figured that even by doing that, I would still hit a homerun or ten that season. I would not be denied.

Throughout the season, I was constantly encouraged to hit to the right side, move the runner along, and on occasion, to bunt.

But when the season was over, I made the City All-Stars again, not the more prestigious State All Star team. I was very disappointed, but there's not much room on the best all-star team for a singles and doubles hitter. My dad was very upset for me, because he knew it was a dream of mine to make the State All-Star team. The new kid made the State All-Stars by hitting four homeruns and pitching to a 4-3 record.

Did the kid's father plot my "failure"? Did he ask me to cut my swing back so his son could shine? Looking back, these are such petty questions.

The lessons were hard, but valuable. By cutting back my swing and advancing runners I learned to be a team player. I played four different positions, led the team in runs, and never complained when I was not allowed to pitch any of the three games against the best team in the league—even though twice it was my turn in the rotation—and who beat us all three times (the new kid pitched those games). As Ty Cobb would say, baseball is not about home runs, it's about helping the team score runs. I hope that somewhere, some day the kid learned the lessons I learned—ironically—from his dad.

The league would let the winning pitcher keep the game ball, and as a pitcher of record, I kept five balls that year. I still have one. We beat the Athletics 8–5. The ball sits on my shelf with my baseball books. It is a reminder of a time when all that was important was wrapped up in cowhide. It was a time when mom and dad (when he was off) would come to see me play regardless of how good we were. My mother would always remind me that God was more important. I said, "I know."

In fact, I never prayed to God as much as when I was at bat, or getting ready to throw the next pitch. But, I don't think that's what she meant. Still, there were moments when I felt closer to God on a baseball field than I ever did in a church. If the New Testament teaches community and love of enemies, then I learned that best as a kid on the baseball field. I learned to rely on my teammates and to trust them. I learned that when they fall, or make an error, they needed support and not ridicule. I learned to love my teammates because we shared a common table, not of food, but of pure, unadulterated fun. We shared a common goal, not winning, but of participation.

We learned that we could say that we hate the Senators, but after they beat us three times for three of our four losses that year we had nothing but respect for them. Somehow, I never learned to respect enemies at church. I learned a lot about hate and divisiveness at church. I learned nothing about a common goal, or a purpose. Not until much later did I ever figure church out. Playing baseball that year, I got a head start on what church was supposed to be.

When I was thirteen I moved up to the Pony League, the thirteen- and fourteen-year-old league. During my two years in this league, there are three moments that stand out.

I played for the Colts. We practiced for about three weeks before the season began. On the day before our first game, Coach Flowers announced who would be starting. Batting ninth and in centerfield would be me. He told me in front of the team that I had hustled more than anyone else on the team and that I deserved my position. He smiled and said, "Good job." That was the best affirmation I ever received while playing baseball. But it was my dad who inspired me to hustle, and not just in Baseball. He urged me to work hard at everything I did. Hustling in Baseball was, however, as natural to me as breathing.

The next night I have no idea if I had a hit or if we won. All I remember is that I caught all three flies in centerfield and backed up second base several times. I remember that night as one of my best baseball moments ever, because I was playing where Dimaggio, Mantle, and Murcer played.

The second moment I remember came the next year. We had a stud on our team. His name was Rickey. And he knew he was a stud. He had no idea what it meant to lose. He had all kinds of talent but he did not have the heart to lose. Some may think that is a good thing. But if you play sports, you better be able to handle loss. Life is just the same.

During a game halfway through the season, Rickey was pitching and was not getting the calls he thought the umpire should be giving. After a while, he walked off. I was playing first base. I could not believe what I saw. He just walked off. The coach couldn't believe it, either. We regrouped, put in another pitcher, and finished the game. After the game we had a team meeting. We kicked him off the team. I don't advocate this action. We should have tried to work it out with him. We gave up on him and shouldn't have.

We had some really good players, and when the all-star team was announced, no one from our team made it. We were told later it was because we kicked Rickey off of our team. Maybe it was harsh to do that to him, but we felt that as a team, we were all in it together, but he was never a true member of our team. He abandoned us. He was picked up by another team and made the all-star team.

The league was set up so that after the all-star team was announced, the league would have a tournament for the whole league to determine the champion. This tournament was played without the all-stars. Since we had no all-stars and we were one of the best teams in the league, we went on to win the championship game, 18-6. We were proud to have no all-stars and to be champions. Team is not about winning; it's about supporting each other and loyalty to a common purpose.

With a championship under my belt, a .400 batting average, and some true seasoning, I was ready for high school baseball.

Steve Williams was the coach of the Bradley Bears. He was 5'4" and was stronger and quicker than anyone I had ever met. When I was a kid, Steve was playing multiple sports at Bradley Central High School. He was a favorite. He was smart on the basketball court, a great playmaker and assist man. He could score when he wanted too, it seemed. He had a reputation of being a hard worker and dedicated to the success of the team. And now, in my freshman year, he would be my coach, but only for a while.

My first day to try out was cold and windy. I changed my clothes in the locker room crowded with the entire returning team and with a lot of freshman hopefuls. This was going to be a real "try" out. Most of us freshman were unknown to Williams. So he let us shag flies in the outfield day after day. Each day he had an assistant to tell us to go to the outfield to catch batting practice. We never got to bat. We had one purpose. To retrieve the fly balls and line drives hit by those on the team.

Day after day the outfield became less crowded. Two hours a day of retrieving balls took its toll. But I would not give up. After about three weeks, and the season around the corner, I finally mustered the courage to ask to bat. Coach Williams said, "Sure."

I was fourteen, soon to be fifteen. I went to get a bat and picked up two or three. Finally, I found a light one. Bat speed would be important. I had not swung a bat for over eight months. What I thought would be batting practice turned into an audition. More realistically, it was an execution.

I stood there and looked up at Keith Mills, an all-county pitcher, soon to be college-bound. The Coach said, "Keith, give him three strikes. Let him hit it."

But out of the corner of my eye I saw the coach make a motion with his hand. Later, I determined that he was telling Mills to give me a curve ball.

Boy, was it. I had never seen anything curve that far. If he had thrown it at my head, two things would have happened. First, I would have fallen on my butt. Second, I would have run home to mama scared to death. I swung while falling backwards.

Strike one.

I did not see if the coach gave a suggestion on the next pitch. Heck, I barely saw the ball. Down the middle with a fastball.

Strike two.

I called time, stepped out, took a breath, and two practice swings.

Mills began his windup and I stood there—barely—with my bat ready and my eyes focused.

The pitch proved one thing: that strike two must have been a change-up. I never saw it. I heard it. But I did not see it. I swung.

Strike three.

"Next," the coach said. "Marc, come here. You will never make it on this team."

I said, "Thanks," and I left.

I will never know if he told me that because he was serious or because he was trying to find out what I was made of.

I may have grown up knowing what it was like to lose, but I had never lost like that. It took me a long time to dress. I was the only one in the locker room. I was too proud to cry in the locker room. (Besides, Tom Hanks told us that there is no crying in baseball.) I rode my bike home and when I got home I could not even remember the trip. My mom asked why I had been crying, but I didn't remember crying. I must have cried on the way home.

I took my shower, ate supper, and, most likely, did my homework. I remember going to my bedroom and looking at my baseball cards. I would never be on a baseball card. And I cried again. I remember that cry. It lasted too long not to remember. For the first time in my life, I asked God a question: "What, then, do you want me to do?"

The answer would not come for four more years.

6

God Went Down to Georgia

> The pitcher has got only a ball. I've got a bat. So the percentage of weapons is in my favor and I let the fellow with the ball do the fretting.
> —Hank Aaron

> When Henry came up, I heard fans yell, "Hit that nigger. Hit that nigger." Henry hit the ball up against the clock. The next time he came up, they said, "Walk him, walk him."
> —Herb Aaron (Hank Aaron's Father)

> You shall have no other gods before me.
> —Exodus 20:3

Looking back at my dad's life, one could say that it was dull, boring. Actually, he lived a calm life, for the most part. He worked a swing-shift job in Chattanooga where they made nylon and other materials. He came home every day, ate his meals, read the paper, he would play catch sometimes, and watch the news. He loved TV. He loved Bob Hope, John Wayne, and he hated to miss *The Fugitive*. Unbelievably, he took a day off to watch the final episode of the *Fugitive*.

But one thing about my dad—he took us on a vacation every summer, even if it was only to the beach. But he also took us to new places. I didn't know it at the time, but Disney World had just opened when he took us to see Mickey and the gang.

In 1966, the Milwaukee Braves settled in Atlanta and baseball had come to the South. My dad took us to a game that very first season. I was only seven, but I still remember that day thanks to a photograph of us standing next to a wall on the ramp going up to our seats. I have no idea who the Braves played or whether they won or lost.

That year the radio was often on in my house, listening to the Braves play. Hank Aaron hit 44 home runs and drove in 127 runs. I became a Braves fan overnight.

Over the years, my dad took us to one or two games each year. Our Little League team also went to one game each year. And there was one reason we went: to see Hank Aaron swing the bat.

And yet, there was something missing about how people talked about Hank: respect. While everyone talked about his power, immediately people only compared him to Mantle or Ruth in light of what he had not done, or how many times it took him to do what he had done. I didn't know what it was at the time, but I could tell that people talked differently about him. It was as if every conversation about Aaron was spoken with verbal asterisks and what was not said was that the reason for this lack of respect was that he was black.

"When he wins five World Series titles, then we can compare him to Mantle," one man said.

Others were not so polite. They used words that were all too commonly heard about a black man in those days, North and South.

Still, there was another conversation going on, one that would become the norm in the future. It was one between me and my friends, teammates, and brothers. We learned baseball from baseball cards and periodicals. With only three networks, no ESPN, and no satellite, we learned all we could about baseball by cards and the *Sporting News*. That paper has been called the sports-lovers bible. And it was. We devoured it. We would buy one and share it for two or three weeks, reading every box score two or three times. We knew that Hank Aaron was special.

There was one day at Fulton County Stadium that I have always remembered. It was a double-header with Pittsburgh. I remember Roberto Clemente, Al Oliver, and Bob Robertson hitting home runs. I remember home runs by a young Darrell Evans and

Mike Lum of the Braves. Phil Niekro of Atlanta and Steve Blass of Pittsburgh pitched.

But the moment that stands out most vividly was the home run that Hank Aaron hit. I can still hear the crack of the bat. When Hank hit the ball it just sounded different. I am sure psychologists might think it is because I expected a special sound, but they would be wrong.

My dad would say that Aaron could not hit those long fly-ball homers that Mantle hit. Some would say that Aaron's home runs barely cleared the fence. And in the short field of Fulton County Stadium, a lot of his home runs were cheap shots. They would say anything to discredit what Aaron was doing.

It's true that many of his home runs barely cleared the fence. But it is also true that Yankee stadium has a closer right field fence down the foul line than should be allowed. Nothing mentioned about that, though.

The reason many of Aaron's home runs barely cleared the fence though was that they were line-drive home runs. They were hit not with raw power like Dave Kingman or Mark McGwire. Rather they were hit like they were shot out of Aaron's bat. It's as if the ball was trying to get as far away from Aaron's bat as soon as possible. Many of those balls barely cleared the fence because they were still on the way up.

At that doubleheader, I remember Hank Aaron's

home run like yesterday. As soon as it was hit, we knew it was gone.

But that was all I remembered. Recently, however, I joined the Society for American Baseball Research (SABR). After I joined, I learned that I now had access to some tremendous research opportunities. I now gained access to the historical archives of the *New York Times* and the *Los Angeles Times*.

So, following thirty years of memory and about fifteen minutes on the Internet, I found the box score to that doubleheader on 23 August 1971. I had turned twelve on 6 August.

In the first game Steve Blass did pitch and it was against Phil Niekro. Pittsburgh won 4-3. Hank Aaron hit his thirty-sixth home run of the year, number 628 of his career. Darrell Evans hit his seventh of the year. The game lasted two hours and eight minutes.

In the second game, Pittsburgh won 15-4. Earl Williams and Mike Lum homered for the Braves. Al Oliver hit two home runs, Bob Robertson hit his twenty-fifth, and Roberto Clemente hit his thirteenth. In October, Pittsburgh would win the World Series over Baltimore.

There were many other games we went to. One year, we went to see the Cincinnati Reds, known as the Big Red Machine. I loved to watch Johnny Bench catch and hit. All my dad could talk about was the hustling of Pete Rose. My dad loved Rose. He truly admired anyone who gave something their all. Rose did that on every play.

I have no idea who the pitchers were, but we were hoping to see some home runs hit by Bench, Foster, Griffey (Sr.), and whoever else wanted to chime in. This night was a pitcher's game. That is, until with two on and two out (I remember my dad complaining about this later.), Joe Morgan stepped up to the plate and hit a line shot over the right field wall. The Reds won 3-0.

Long after Aaron had retired, and I was a hybrid Yankees/Braves fan, my favorite player was Bobby Murcer. He was the heir apparent to Mickey Mantle and Joe DiMaggio. Talk about pressure. Murcer was a very good player on the biggest stage in sports. Yet, he was never the superstar people wanted him to be. I liked him and liked to watch him hit and field.

As much as I love the Yankees I almost gave them up the day I picked up the *Chattanooga Free Press* out of our yard and the sports headline announced that the Yankees had traded Murcer for Bobby Bonds. It was like getting hit in the gut.

But over the winter it dawned on me that while this was not the best trade in the world, Murcer and the Giants would have to visit Atlanta. I would finally get to see him play in person. There's nothing like going zero for four to sour an evening, but I still saw him play.

But the thing is that my dad took me. He knew it meant the world to me to see Murcer play. How could he not when I asked him about it every day? But he took the time to take me, and that is all that matters.

Baseball in Atlanta is a great thing. Now, there are two more teams in the South, both in Florida. Why is there no team in North Carolina or Tennessee? But we do have the Braves. When I was in Little League we would talk about our favorite teams and players. I had one friend who loved the Pirates. His great-uncle had once been a coach with them. But most of us loved our Braves. And despite the way our dads and coaches and sportswriters would talk about Hank Aaron, we talked about him as if he were nothing but a baseball player. We cared nothing about the color of his skin. We didn't even notice it until someone pointed it out. What we saw was a guy with more than 500 home runs, then more than 600 home runs, and then 700 home runs.

Then, on 4 April 1974, Hank "went and done it." He hit number 715. I was so excited, so thrilled. They were talking about placing an asterisk beside his home run total because it took him hundreds of at bats more than Ruth, but that's not why they wanted the asterisk. Like when Maris broke the single season home run record, they simply did not want Ruth's record broken. With Aaron, it was worse. It wasn't simply nostalgia. They didn't want a black man to break Ruth's record. Heck, they didn't want any black man to break any record.

Many people talk about the courage of Jackie Robinson, and yes, he did have courage. And his talents and accomplishments speak for themselves. But Hank Aaron did more, and he did it in the even more hostile environment of the South. Brooklyn was no picnic for Robinson, either. Racism does not know geography. With daily threats on his life and the lives of his family from bigoted and ruthless (no pun) individuals, and in the midst of the Civil Rights Movement, Hank Aaron was the best baseball player of his generation—arguably, of all time.

Martin Luther King Jr. was in the news in those days, and he was making headlines and fueling a revolution. But from my perspective, Aaron did as much with his bat as King did with his speeches.

At the Pirates doubleheader that day, a pastor seated near us called Aaron a "little n----- boy." All I could think of was the song: "Red or yellow, black or white, they are precious in his sight." Aaron was called a lot of things by fans and enemies. My friends and I thought he was a god. Aaron's autobiography is titled *I Had a Hammer*. Maybe he was the incarnation of Thor.

And he was in Georgia.

7

Baptism

> I must admit, when Reggie hit his third home run (1977 World Series) and I was sure nobody was looking, I applauded in my glove.
> —Steve Garvey

> There is a river that makes glad the city of God.
> —Psalm 46

Growing up following the Yankees was not what my dad led me to expect. When I was young, the Yankees were not what they once were. From 1965 until 1975 they were mediocre at best. St. George (Steinbrenner) rode in to slay the dragon with his checkbook, and yes, eventually, championships would come. But from age six until age sixteen, I had little to cheer about except when Bobby Murcer hit four consecutive home runs in a doubleheader against Cleveland, or when he chased the batting crown one year. And then, in 1974, after Steinbrenner said that Murcer would be there as long as he owned the team, he traded my hero.

Then 1976 came. It was a different team. Thurman Munson was the heart and soul of the squad. Hitting .302, 17 home runs, and 105 runs batted in, Munson led the team at bat and in the field. Graig Nettles hit 32 home runs, and with Chris Chambliss, Roy White, Lou Pinella, Mickey Rivers, and Willie Randolph, the Yankees won 97 games and went to the World Series for the first time in my memory. With Catfish Hunter (seventeen wins), Ed Figueroa (nineteen wins), Dock Ellis (seventeen wins), Ken Holtzman (fourteen wins), and Doyle Alexander (thirteen wins), the Yankees had a great starting rotation. Plus, in the bullpen they had Sparky Lyle. Of course, they lost to the Big Red Machine, the Cincinnati Reds, in the World Series 4-0. I was a crushed senior in high school.

The Yankees were two players short of a World Series championship. Fateful 1977 would find those two players. The first was "Louisiana Lightning," aka Ron Guidry. In 1977, he would go 16-7. With Mike Torrez, Figueroa, Don Gullett, Dick Tidrow, and Hunter, the Yankees had radically changed their pitching rotation from the season before. But Guidry's presence was a key ingredient.

The second player added was more flamboyant and controversial. "If I play in New York, they will name a candy bar after me." So said Reggie Jackson. Signed as a free agent, my dad almost stopped rooting for the Yankees because of Jackson. Only Munson's presence on the team kept him from hating all the Yankees. He cared nothing for Steinbrenner after trading Murcer and signing Jackson.

Jackson talked a lot. He also backed it up. That year, 1977, the Yankees won 100 games. In October, they played the Dodgers in the World Series.

The Yankees were ahead in the series 3 games to 2; the date was 17 October 1977. It was a date I will never forget. It was the night by dad got baptized.

As we sat down to watch the game I noticed that my dad was quieter than usual. Something was on his mind. Actually, I thought maybe he had been drinking and was just phasing out. But he had not been drinking. We chatted briefly about the game, and about our day.

Mom went to bed early that night. Dad and I watched the game together. I was eighteen years old. I lay on the couch, and he sat in the chair. Reggie came to bat. He homered and my dad made no comment. That the Yankees would win meant more than his dislike of Jackson. He had always said that he never had respect for anyone who talked about how great they are and about how bad others were. That is what he thought of Jackson. My dad was a very modest, humble man and would never brag on himself. Consequently, he did not have much respect for anyone else who bragged. Thus, he taught me that bragging had no place in a person's life. As a comparison and a contrast, he thought Munson was the ideal ballplayer.

After Jackson's second homer of the game, my dad got up and shook his head. It must have been killing him. Jackson had just tied the record for home runs in a World Series (four), and the Yankees were fast on their way to winning their first series since 1962 when they beat the Giants four games to three.

He came back in the room and sat down. He started talking. "Marc, I know I have not been the best Christian. But I have tried to live a good life and be a good father."

Where this was coming from I had no idea. We rarely talked so deep about anything.

"But I want you to know that I am a Christian. I was saved," he stammered.

"When?" was all I could say.

"When I was fourteen, fifteen, or sixteen, I don't really remember," he mustered. "We were having a revival and I asked Jesus to come into my heart."

"I bet your parents were happy," I said, knowing that my grandfather was preaching the revival and that my grandmother was one of the most vocal church members to have ever lived.

"They never knew," he responded. "Mother was pulling at me and shouting and praying out loud that I would go down front and be saved. She wanted me too, but I just couldn't do it. I stayed right there and clutched the pew in front of me." But once the invitation was over, I closed my eyes and prayed to God, and I became a Christian."

"You never told them?" I asked, unbelieving.

"No. And I was never baptized. But I don't think God ever minded that, do you?"

"Baptism is for others to see what God has already done," I said, suddenly wiser than my years.

Then my dad cried. He cried hard for what seemed like several minutes until he regained his composure.

"I never told anyone that before," he said.

"Neither will I," I said. And I didn't until I preached his funeral.

He stood up and said good night, baptized by his own tears.

I lay there stunned. The game was still on. Bob Welch was pitching for the Dodgers. Reggie was up again. The pitch. The crack. Home run number three for the night, number five for the series. They called him Mr. October.

I stayed up late watching the celebration. I was raised a Yankees fan, and now, for the first time in my life that I could remember, the Yankees had won the World Series. The Yankee players and coaches and even George Steinbrenner were sharing champagne and drowning one another. They were immersed in victory.

Thinking about the conversation with my dad, I realized what life was truly about. For one night, everything was right. I never thought anything would make me happier than the Yankees winning the World Series. That night, I learned differently. The most personal conversation I ever had with my dad showed me that.

Now, whenever someone mentions, or I see it on my shelf, Will Campbell's *The Glad River* has a very personal meaning for me. When I first read that book and how Doops Momber was never baptized, I thought of my dad. There's always room in the Glad River, the river that runs through the city of God (Ps 46), for anyone who never found a seat in church.

8

Home Run

> Please God, let me hit one. I'll tell everybody you did it.
> —Reggie Jackson

> I thank my God upon every remembrance of you.
> —Philippians 1:3

In 1978, two things happened that forever changed my life. I was a fairly boring person. But I never thought much about it. I attended church, loved baseball, and had started college. I worked part-time and had plenty to keep me busy. I never stayed out late. I never got into trouble.

My mom and I began going to a new church. Being Baptist in the South is as natural as peanut butter and jelly, and just as messy. But we had a new church home and I began to change for the better. My mom was always the anchor of our home. With dad working odd hours, he left all of our school and church and just about anything else up to her. She made sure my brothers and I were in church from the time we were toddlers, or an infant in my case. No mother ever loved her children more than mine.

But when she and I began going to a different church we found a different view of God that we had never known before. We fit right in and loved it. During that first year, I struggled with my own future. I had started college taking general education courses, but did not have a clue what to do about a major or even a career. I went to a career day program and sat in on a thirty-minute discussion on being an accountant. I could not get out of there fast enough.

While at this new church, Westwood Baptist, I became involved in a wonderful Sunday school class, and attended Wednesday night and Sunday night services. The more I was there the more I needed it. It was a great place to be.

As naïve as I was, I began to think that God was trying to get my attention. My mom and I started a reading-the-Bible-through-in-a-year program. This opened my world to reading something other than baseball cards and schoolbooks. I began to love reading. I never suspected that one day I would be in publishing.

One night, when my parents were on a weekend

vacation—a rare thing—I finally "knew" what was wanted of me. I picked up my Bible and asked God what he wanted. I randomly opened my Bible to Ephesians 3:7 that reads in part, "For this reason, I became a minister...." God was calling me to the ministry. That was the first thing.

It's a funny thing about "being called" by God. You are the only witness. Everyone will believe you if you live it. But if you ever do anything wrong, everyone will let you know that a "called" person does not do such things. So, when God calls, you have to be sure.

I was sure. God wanted me to be a youth minister, or a preacher. Actually, I was sure of the call, but I was not as sure of what to. After I started seminary that call would change twice after I arrived. But when I graduated it would change a third time.

The second thing was that if God was busy with me, then that sure explained why the Yankees, after winning the World Series the year before, were fourteen games out of first place.

While I was struggling to find my way in life, the Yankees were having a dreadful season. Not in wins, necessarily. It was the Red Sox that made the season long. The Red Sox were in first place and looked like they could beat not only the '78 Yankees, but that they could handle the immortal '27 Yankees. But, by season's end, Ron Guidry would be 25-3, with a 1.74

ERA, pitch sixteen complete games, and throw nine shutouts. It was a dream season for Guidry. Guidry was one of my favorite players, and the only baseball player I ever had a poster of on the wall next to my bed. (I could never find Mantle, Aaron, or Murcer posters.) That year, the left-hander was awesome. No one wanted to face him. With Ed Figueroa (20-9, 2.99 ERA), the two pitchers formed an unstoppable duo.

Offensively, Jackson's home runs were down a bit and he and Graig Nettles tied for the team lead at twenty-seven. Not a single Yankee drove in more than ninety-seven runs, and not a single player scored more than eighty-seven. But when push came to shove, the Yankees did the unthinkable. They fought back after the all-star break and made a run at the pennant.[1]

On the last day of the season, the Yankees had tied the Red Sox for first place in the Eastern division. A one-game playoff would decide the champion. They would play at Fenway Park.

On 2 October 1978 the Yankees played the Red Sox in one of the most exciting games ever played. I am sure Red Sox fans don't remember the day fondly. But others remember it well. The Yankees had fought back from a fourteen-game deficit under the leadership of Bob Lemon, following the midseason

---

[1] This story is best told by Roger Kahn in his book, *October Men: Reggie Jackson, George Steinbrenner, Billy Martin, and the Yankees' Miraculous Finish in 1978* (New York: Harcourt, 2003).

firing of Billy Martin as manager. Guidry was 24-3 going into that playoff game.

Guidry pitched on three days rest against Mike Torrez, who had pitched for the Yankees the year before. Guidry had lost only three games, each to a different pitcher named Mike.

While Yaz, Lynn, Rice, and Burleson led the Red Sox, Munson, Jackson, and Nettles led the Yankees. It was Bucky Dent, however, who was the difference that day. Trailing 2-0, with two on, Dent stepped up and hit a three-run home run. Jackson added a home run later. The Yankees won 5-4 with Goose Gossage getting Yaz out with runners on in the bottom of the ninth.

The curse of the bambino was still on. Ever since the Red Sox sold Babe Ruth to the Yankees in 1918 the Red Sox had not won a single World Series while the Yankees had won more than twenty. I thought God must have worn pinstripe underwear. (Yes, the Red Sox won it all in 2004, breaking the "curse." But you know what they say about monkeys with typewriters in a room and Shakespeare.")

The playoffs went as hoped and the Yankees returned to the World Series to face, once again, the Dodgers. On Tuesday, 10 October 1978, the Dodgers won 11-5. They won again the next day, 4-3. Both games were played in Los Angeles.

Things had to get better when they went back to

New York. Things did. On Friday the thirteenth, the Yankees won 5-1 behind Guidry's complete game. It was the only game he would pitch in the series, but if they had lost game 6, he would have pitched game 7.

On Saturday, baseball was no longer as important. In the movie *Good Will Hunting*, Robin Williams plays a psychology professor trying to help Matt Damon's character. He tells the young man about the night Carlton Fisk and the Red Sox were playing the Reds in the World Series at Fenway. It was game 6 and he had a ticket to that game when Fisk hit that incredible, unforgettable home run. But the psych-professor didn't see it. He did not even attended the game. Why? He said he had to "see about a girl."

On Saturday, 14 October 1978, before the game, I went to the mall. I used to love to go to the mall. Other than going to the movies, there was not a lot to do in Cleveland, Tennessee. I had a couple of friends who worked at different stores in the mall and I would go by to say hello, sometimes to eat lunch or supper. I would visit the bookstore and the record store, back when they had 8-track tapes.

My friend Danny worked in a shoe store. I would often go by to see him and we would talk about music and girls, girls and music. Not much variety, but entertaining nonetheless. Danny's mother managed the card shop across from the shoe store. On this afternoon, Danny was not working, but as I left the store I glanced into the card shop and saw a young woman sitting at the counter. She was very attractive. I walked by and waved and muttered something of a hello. Later, I came back and went in and met Susan Baker. It was one of those moments that changes your life. Why did I do it? I had seen attractive ladies before and never tried to meet them. Why then? After I went in, we chatted for a while and I left. I can't remember what we said or what she wore. But I do remember her eyes.

That night, the Yankees won game four 4-3. The series was tied 2-2. The next day after church I found myself driving to the mall to talk to Susan again. It was late in the afternoon and a home for kids who had either troubled parents or no parents at all had brought the kids to the mall. Some of the kids were in the card shop, and one of them—he was around ten or so—was trying to make Susan his girlfriend. The number one rule of engagement is to not underestimate the enemy. Since I was bigger and stronger and I had a car, I knew the advantage was mine. I was also smarter, by virtue of age alone. Nonetheless, by the end of the afternoon, he went home empty, and I went home with her phone number.

Susan was staying with friends of her parents or we might have had our first date that night. As it was, we would have to wait until the next Saturday. After my triumphant afternoon, the Yankees won that night, 12-2.

On Tuesday night, the Yankees won 7-2 behind the pitching of Catfish Hunter. Mr. October, Reggie Jackson, hit another home run, once again off Bob Welch. The Yankees had lost the first two games and then reeled off four consecutive wins. Bucky Dent was the MVP of the series. Some suggested that while Jackson was Mr. October, Dent earned the title for that year.

All week long I was elated. And the Yankees were not the reason. I could not wait for Saturday night. Saturday finally came after several phone calls Susan and I shared that week. On Saturday morning, my dad and I got ready to go to Knoxville to watch the Tennessee and Alabama football game. It was a cool, windy day and Alabama beat Tennessee, again. The ride home was long, but I cared nothing about the game. I only cared about getting home, showering, and picking up Susan for our first date.

We went to the Jaycees Haunted House. There is no better first date than going to a haunted house. It did not take long to find us holding hands. Her hand felt like silk.

I took her home, and kissed her gently.

The kiss may have been "first base," but I knew I had hit a home run. It was the greatest moment of my life. Two and one-half years later we would be married.

Sorry Reggie and Bucky. That year I was Mr. October.

9

The Promised Land

> A ballpark at night is more like a church than a church.
> —W. P. Kinsella, *Shoeless Joe*

> We climbed, he first and I behind, until, through a small round opening ahead of us I saw the lovely things the heavens hold, and we came out to see once more the stars.
> —Dante *Inferno*, 33:136–139 (Musa)

Susan and I were married on 30 May 1981. I had been out of college all of three weeks. On our wedding night we turned the television on to the Braves game for one-half of an inning so we could tell people we watched the Braves that night.

For the first three weeks of marriage we lived

with my parents. Then we moved to Louisville, Kentucky, so I could attend seminary and get my Master of Religious Education (MRE) degree. Seminary was a great time. My very first course was on Amos with Page Kelley, a man whose life would shape my own during my entire time at seminary and eventually he influenced me in my departure years later.

The MRE degree was a two-year program. I planned to get in, get out, and start working in a church. God and the fundamentalists had other ideas.

At the end of my first year, I felt God pulling me to become a pastor. I grew to love biblical studies and church history to the extent that I knew my gift of loving these things would never be satisfied as a youth minister. I felt my gifts being shaped in my classes.

I changed to the Master of Divinity (M.Div.) degree and took Hebrew in the fall with John Joseph Owens. He literally wrote the book on biblical Hebrew (published by Harper & Row). I loved it. I could not get enough of it. The day we began reading the book of Jonah in Hebrew was one of the most exciting days of my seminary-life.

As my studies progressed, I began to think about doctoral work. I had had classes with Glenn Hinson, Bill Leonard, and Timothy George for Church History and loved history. I also loved Hebrew and the Old Testament.

It was the early 1980s and one demonic cloud hung over the seminary: the fundamentalists were taking over the Southern Baptist Convention. It's a long story,[2] but as the years went by, more and more professors were leaving voluntarily before the witch hunters came oxymoronically with their torches and King James Bibles, complete with their naïve and exclusivistic hermeneutics.

Since Glenn Hinson had departed, Bill Leonard was on sabbatical, and Timothy George told me he was leaving soon, I was more than happy to try for a place in Old Testament graduate school. In order to go further and follow God's "revised call" to teaching, I promised Susan that she could go to school. She entered the University of Louisville School of Nursing.

I made application for the Ph.D. program. I took the MAT, the GRE, and filled out all the papers. I talked to Tom Smothers about studying history with him and he seemed agreeable. I would mix my love of history with my love of the Old Testament. Perfect.

But those test scores were not so good. When I made application for the Ph.D. program I knew there was a chance that I would first have to do a two-year Master of Theology (Th.M.). But I would not mind at all as I believed the extra work would be advantageous.

The letter came in late November 1984 saying

---

[2] Best told by David Morgan, *The New Crusades, the New Holy Land: Conflict in the Southern Baptist Convention, 1969–1991* (Tuscaloosa: University of Alabama Press, 1996).

that I was accepted for the Th.M. program. After graduation exercises, I saw Dr. Kelley and shook his hand. He asked a question I did not fully hear at first. He asked what were my plans. Well, I told him, I was looking forward to the graduate program with him and the other department members. He politely told me he wished me the best.

Three days later he sent me a note saying he needed to see me. I went to his office and he had one of those talks that I am sure he dreaded. While I was accepted in the Th.M. program, there simply was no room for me in the OT department for any more students. My acceptance, however, was premature. We had a good talk.

Just before leaving, I casually mentioned, without any hope at all, that I was confused because Dr. Smothers had agreed to let me study with him, but that I appreciated his help. I was crushed. And, that day, there was no bike to speed me home.

I went home for a long day, longer than the day I stopped playing baseball. I was unsure of not only my academic future, but also of my now imminent departure from campus housing.

The next day Dr. Smothers called. He had talked with Dr. Kelley and, if I still wanted to, I could start the Th.M. the next fall. Words fail me in describing my reaction. For twenty hours I was faced with having to find a job and a new place to live within two weeks, to now being granted a chance to pursue my "call" to teach. Whatever they discussed, I will never forget their act of grace and kindness.

It did not quite work out as planned. I studied not with Dr. Smothers but with Dr. Pamela Scalise. I do not regret it at all. She was wonderful to work with and I was one of her first grad students.

My thesis was on the hermeneutics of Brevard Childs, with whom Pam studied with at Yale. After my thesis defense, my committee asked for lots of revisions. Based on those revisions they would determine whether I would enter the Ph.D. program. At my oral defense, Dr. Marvin Tate, a member of my committee, said that I had shown good improvement, but the revisions would be critical.

I spent about two weeks on the revisions, as the deadline approached. I turned it in and passed. But how good were the rewrites?

Several weeks later, I went to find out. It had been too long and I assumed the worst. I went to see Dr. Scalise and, surprised, she asked if I had received a letter from Dr. Tate.

I had not, and so I went to see him.

After the long walk down the hall and up the stairs, Dr. Tate told me that I would be in the Ph.D. program on the condition that he supervise my work. They had simply forgotten to contact me. Fine by me. Like baseball, grad school (like life) is full of bad bounces. Every now and then one bounces your way. For a while I thought I was Tony Kubek getting hit in the throat by a bad bounce in the World Series more than twenty years earlier. When Bill Buckner got no bounce in 1986 against the Mets I never blamed him. Sometimes life gives you a bad bounce and sometimes it gives you no bounce and sometimes it comes as easy as a slow roller with the catcher trying to run it out.

In the meantime I had been teaching at Simmons University Bible College, an African-American school in Louisville of about 100 students. The pay was one tenth of normal pay for teaching, but the place was wonderful. I taught there for six years. Being only one of four whites in the school—three of us were instructors—was the best learning experience I could have had. First, I was accepted unconditionally. I learned how to teach. I came to know the students and respected them. Most of them believed they were following God's call. Some really struggled, like the guy who missed every third class. When I asked him why, he said some days he only had enough gas to get to work or school, and he had to choose. I learned that he was telling the truth.

Isaiah White was a bright, inquisitive, and warmhearted student. He had a great sense of humor. During my second year, he was in my philosophy of religion class. Someone asked about racial issues in Cleveland when I was a boy. I shared some stories about things I was lied to about and told about African Americans, and, in good humor, added, "It was tough growing up white in the South." Smiling from ear to ear, Isaiah responded, "You should have tried it being black. Right, Dr. Jolley?"

"Isaiah, you know I don't have my doctorate yet. But I do have a masters degree, so you can call me master." The class erupted and he called me master the rest of the day.

After six years, I left Simmons and have always wanted to return. I taught for the pure love of teaching. Teaching there taught me more about love and community than I have learned anywhere else other than the baseball field.

The Ph.D. program is too long and boring to go into detail. I could tell about the semester I wrote more than 200 pages in papers and translations, or the summer I was sick with a nervous stomach and read all the writings of René Girard, or how I grew to love Aramaic. Or how I struggled through French and German. I could tell about the exams between the coursework and the dissertation. And then, there is the dissertation itself.

What was most troubling during this time, however, was how all this was received by my parents and brothers and in-laws. Why was I doing this? Didn't I start out trying to become a youth minister? Why a Ph.D.? Being the only person in my family who attended college for any length of time was a feat. But to have gone on to seminary was noble and

Christian. But now, continuing on seemed a bit much.

I worked four part-time jobs during grad school. Susan worked, also, as a phlebotomist and as a nursing assistant. How did we survive? We had little, but had all we needed and then some. Susan and I have always been hard workers. Emotionally we had each other. But for relaxation there was always Cave Hill cemetery—where we would walk around, feed the geese, or sit and read. And, there was baseball.

Louisville was the home to the St. Louis Cardinals' farm team, the Louisville Redbirds. We saw Willie McGee, Vince Coleman, and numerous players come through. But the truth of the matter is that I saw a lot of games because of Rusty Cherry, a friend who was also in the Ph.D. OT program. We spent our free time going to flea markets to hunt baseball cards, playing intramural softball and basketball, and going to baseball games. One summer he, his wife Betsy, Susan, and I took a vacation to St. Louis to see his favorites—the Cardinals—play the Mets. We sat in right field and watched Darryl Strawberry that night.

Once each spring the Cardinals would come to Louisville for an exhibition and time to meet with the fans. I will never forget two consecutive seasons. The first was the year that Tommy Herr sat by himself and would not sign anything. The next year he mixed in with everyone and signed until no one was left. It seems in the off-season, he met Christ.

We also went to Cincinnati for games on occasion. It seems that baseball was the best way to find my way. I was constantly bombarded with Hebrew grammar and nothing offset it like trading cards or watching a game.

As I finished the doctoral program and began writing my dissertation—"The Function of Torah in Sirach" (don't ask)—I realized that finding a teaching job would be very difficult. The Baptist colleges that used to hire students from Southern Seminary were looking elsewhere. The Fundamentalist-Moderate controversy was taking its toll. There were simply very few jobs. Being a white male Baptist at the time put me in the extreme minority. That was a bad bounce.

After sending out more than seventy applications and having only one interview at Ouachita Baptist University, things looked as bad as my dissertation was looking. After much prayer and looking for answers I turned to the book. I had grown to love books. I adored books. It was not financially healthy. But after thinking about my situation I turned to the book. No, not the Bible. I turned to *What Color Is Your Parachute?* That's the book that helps you find what you are qualified to do with your life. I read what a person with a religious degree could do, and there it was: editor. It was as clear to me as the day I read from Ephesians and I knew that God wanted me to be a youth minister. Although, looking back it was really not that clear.

I began thinking about being an editor. I told no one about my consulting this book, but I thought about it for two weeks. And then the phone rang. Tom Clark at Broadman and Holman in Nashville wanted to know if I would be interested in a job editing academic books. I was. Page Kelley had recommended me for the job. The ball bounced my way. Or did it?

This was great, but the Baptist Fundamentalists had already secured the doors to the Baptist Sunday School Board, but many inside were not of that persuasion. I interviewed with Tom Clark and Linda Scott—she would be my Nashville mom and friend for three years—and when they offered me the job I took it. Some of my close friends criticized me for going, but my friend and boss Chris Conver supported me and encouraged me. He said the experience would be good for me. It was not "good," but it did prove to be beneficial as my entrance into a profession—publishing—that I love.

One week before we left, Dr. Tate walked in the back door of the bookstore, handed me my dissertation, and told me I needed to rewrite it. The transition to Nashville would not be an easy one. I thought I finally knew what Bill Buckner felt. I was in the World Series, but the world just caved in. As in all things, it's not the bounce, bad or good, that determines your life. Its how you handle it the next morning you wake up.

Eleven years after we arrived in Louisville, me nearly with a Ph.D. and Susan with her BSN we headed to Nashville. For the first nine and one-half years in Louisville we were happy, but not until our son John Patrick was born did we feel like we had been touched by God's very hand. While we were very happy before his birth, he elevated our joy to a new level. I count him my second home run, but I had help this time.

Those years in Louisville were spent studying about God and trying to get the Yankees back to the World Series. That first fall in Louisville they did go back in the worst baseball season ever: the strike season. They lost to the Dodgers four games to two. They would not get back to the World Series until 1996, despite what Don Mattingly promised years before.

We moved to Nashville, Tennessee, in 1992. We took Patrick to see the Nashville Sounds play and all I recall is that he was upset that he could not get on the field with them and play. I finally completed my dissertation in the fall of 1993. I had started seminary in 1981 when Duke McCall was president, had been a student throughout all of Roy Honeycutt's tenure, and would finish in the first weeks of the fundamentalist and chauvinistic rule of the Albert

Mohler, a former classmate. I may be one of but a few students in the history of Southern Baptist Theological Seminary who was a student during the terms of three consecutive presidents. Regardless, our life in Louisville was wonderful.

We moved to Macon, Georgia, in 1995, home of the Macon Braves. Between the Louisville Redbirds, the Nashville Sounds, and the Macon Braves, we had selected good places to watch minor league ball.

Broadman and Holman had been a mixed blessing. I met some great people there. I worked with an unbelievably excellent staff. We had bought a house, I had taught a class at Belmont University, we had a great church family, but soon it—the Sunday School Board policies and theology—wore me down. I had to get out. But without my time there I would never have landed the job at Mercer University Press.

It was in Nashville that I had one of the darkest moments of my life. It may be the subject for another book, but for the extra year I had to rewrite my dissertation, I began to slowly slip into melancholia. Depression is too strong and too clinical. Melancholia is a better word. Looking back without the help of any medical or psychological help, I cannot pinpoint why I experienced it, but I often think it had more to do with the fact that I now worked at an organization that had gone through the same transformation as Southern Seminary. While I had left Southern, I had not left the devastatingly

A Memoir of God, Baseball, and Family 101

exclusivistic, chauvinistic, and dogmatic actions of the people now in control of the Southern Baptist Convention. Coupled with this, Susan and I had just bought our first house, and the mortgage was like a noose around my neck. This melancholia only needed the right ambience to settle over me, and that winter, we had an ice storm. While the melancholia had been coming on for a few weeks, the ice storm forced me to send Susan and Patrick to stay with my parents for a few days, leaving me alone. While I stayed with some friends waiting for the electricity to be restored, it was truly *winter* for me.

I found myself at a bookstore and happened upon a book by William Styron, *Darkness Visible*. (Charles Breslin had recommended this book years before.) Styron's memoir of his battle with depression is one of the books that changed my life. While he was battling depression and contemplated suicide (I never did), he finally found purpose—his family. He emerged from his depression, in the words of Dante, "to see the stars." Styron helped me to *see the stars*. I slowly emerged from the melancholia and learned that family should be my priority. I remember thinking that I would love to meet his family, especially his kids, who had been the reason he survived his depression.

I needed to leave Nashville. Marvin Tate asked me if I had heard about a job at Mercer University Press. I had not. I applied and was offered the job. My new boss said one thing that convinced me: "There is freedom here." That's all I needed to hear. I looked at my time in Nashville as my minor league training. I was going to the show.

I arrived at my new job on September 8, 1995. A few weeks later, Tom Glavine pitched eight shutout innings, backed by a David Justice homerun, and the Braves were world champions. Life was good. I had a great job. I liked the big leagues.

One thing lingered: what about that call? Had not God called me to teach? Or was it to youth ministry, or to preach? What was that experience about that night when I was sitting on my bed reading Paul's words from Ephesians 3:7: "for this Gospel I was made a minister...." But in the NRSV the word is "servant," not "minister." The same Greek word, but different translations. I believed in that call. I believed it the night I was told by a church that they had selected someone else as their pastor; I believed it the day that Ouachita Baptist University picked someone else to teach Old Testament; I believed it throughout my graduate work; I believed it while I was at Broadman and Holman; and I believed it when I accepted the job at Mercer University Press. Then why did I never land a teaching job?

I have taught since 1986 as an adjunct at several schools. When I think about it, I have taught Sunday school since 1980. I guess I have been a teacher longer than I realized. My problem is that I confused employment with calling.

Now, I often teach as an adjunct at Mercer University. I teach classes at churches on film and faith, on television and faith, on books and faith. I think my problem is that I have been too busy teaching to realize that the calling is being fulfilled. It's a bit like a baseball player from the '50s whose name I have forgotten. He was hitting something like .350 and second in the league in home runs, and a sportswriter who asked him about his batting average was interviewing him. The player said, "What is it, anyway?"

"Don't you know?" responded the writer.

"I've no idea," the player replied.

Sometimes I have been too concerned with the logistics that I missed the action. It would be a bit like sitting down in the media booth at a ballgame and keeping statistics so frantically that you would miss the game. It's not a good thing to be so consumed with finding the calling that I missed the game I was called to play.

In Macon, we found the home we had been looking for. Still, something was missing. In 2000, we found it: our second son, David. Home run number three. David is full of life and is a very animated boy.

One day, Susan mentioned that Patrick needed

some special time with his dad. Not long after 9/11, she suggested that Patrick and I go on a trip together. Cool, I thought. She even suggested a baseball trip. That was cooler still.

That November we started talking about where we would like to go in June for our trip. We discussed Camden Yards in Baltimore since it was only about eleven hours away. We talked about going to see games in Texas, St. Louis, Cincinnati, Chicago, and even Tampa Bay. Patrick was not too keen on flying. But as we checked schedules, we could not find a time in June or July that had the team matchups we wanted in those cities.

Of course, New York is the only place I wanted to go, but did not even consider it until Patrick suggested that he would be willing to fly. Since he was a Diamondbacks fan we thought of going to Arizona, but still the matchups were not what we wanted. Just for the heck of it we checked New York for Yankee games in June. And there it was: the perfect scenario. On 9 June they were playing the Giants. Patrick really wanted to see Barry Bonds. And on 10 June, the Yankees had the rematch from the previous World Series with Patrick's favorite team, the Diamondbacks. We were headed to the Promised Land.

On 1 December 2001, the Mercer University Press authors luncheon was held in Atlanta. At the dinner the night before, I sat next to an author and her husband. They lived in New York City. Her name was Alexandra Styron, and I told her how her father's book had changed my life.

On 8 June 2002, Patrick and I went to the airport on a shuttle service. He was nervous. He had never flown before, and such experiences can be terrifying for an eleven-year-old. I had prepared him for the problems he might have with his ears, but until you have flown the first time, there is no way to prepare mentally.

He was not thrilled with the plane. He patiently endured it. I thought he was okay. But apparently he was nervous. He rarely shows his feelings.

He was relieved when the plane landed. We got our bags and found a taxi to take us to West 79th Street to the Excelsior Hotel. Our cab ride was unbelievable. I was so excited to see the sights; I did not notice how bad the guy was driving. He was fast and swervy and careless. He was in a hurry. Patrick's nerves were at their end anyway. The drive moved them to a new level, so Patrick left the guy a present in the back floorboard. His stomach could not handle it and started to back up. I tried to catch it in a bag that had our muffins in it, but most landed on my leg and my Yankees hat.

We got out of the cab and I paid the fare and apologized. We went inside our hotel, got cleaned up, and then had four of the best days of our lives.

Our hotel was across the street from the American Museum of Natural History, and only a half block from Central Park.

We headed up to 81st Street to eat at the Jackson Hole. We had awesome hamburgers. Then we visited the Barnes & Noble Bookstore three blocks over for about two hours. We left and found where the subway was closest to our hotel and walked around Theodore Roosevelt Park next to the museum.

We went to sleep that night in pure excitement. Not only were we going to Yankee Stadium the next day, but also we were going to see Roger Clemens pitch to Barry Bonds, their first major league encounter.

We woke the next morning and got ready. My Yankee's hat was a navy blue one and I knew I needed a white hat since our seats were in the upper deck in left field. We got our stuff and headed for the subway. When we got off at 161st Street, we took a moment for a picture. I had Patrick stand under the Yankee Stadium sign in the subway and I took his photograph. Then we went up the stairs and emerged in the Bronx. Immediately before us there was a McDonalds unlike any I had ever seen. It was a Yankees McDonalds. We went in, looked at all the memorabilia, and then left.

We went out, turned one block and there was the temple of baseball: Yankee Stadium. I just stood there and looked at it. It was not quite an epiphany, but it felt like one. If I had ever had doubts about my employment and my calling to the ministry or to teaching, at that moment I knew I was supposed to be there at that moment in time. I recalled in *Field of Dreams* when Shoeless Joe Jackson, after taking batting practice from Ray Kinsella, asked Ray, "Is this heaven?"

While Yankee Stadium is not quite heaven—in fact, it is a most hated and dreaded place to many—I found heaven a little closer in that moment. It is not in a place. You cannot say "Look, there it is" or "Here it is." Rather, it was within my experience. It was a happiness similar to that I had felt when Susan said "yes" and then eighteen months later "I do." It was similar to when I held Patrick and David for the first time. It was like the time Danny Glover asks Kevin Kline at the end of *Grand Canyon*, "What do you think?" and Kline responded, "I think it's not all bad."

Just seeing the outside of the stadium with my own eyes validated all my love of a game that despite all of its faults had shaped much of who I am.

"C'mon, dad," I heard Patrick say.

I started moving again, and breathing, too. You can see pictures of something all your life, but never will you see it unless you are there in person. Like the Sistine Chapel ceiling painted by Michelangelo, I didn't understand it until I was in that chapel looking up and finally figured it out.

We walked hurriedly toward the stadium, even though we arrived an hour before the gates opened. I guess I should have found out what time they opened, but the place was already busy with people anxious to get in. There were gift shops and hot dog stands everywhere. I bought a white Yankees cap, but what we needed was a portable air conditioner and some sunscreen. The sun was high and it was hot.

While we waited, Patrick sat down and started reading a Redwall novel and I took his picture. Being a lover of books and baseball, I took the picture with the words "Yankee Stadium" showing in the background. How many kids would take time to read a book in a place and time like this. And I felt like I was his age. Right then I promised myself that one day I would return and bring David.

Finally, we were allowed in. It was a complete sellout. We entered the aisle and stopped to take another photograph of our first time in the stadium with the field spread out behind us. A man offered to take a picture of both of us and we quickly accepted his offer. The field was beautiful. It was all I had seen on TV and more.

Kinsella said that baseball parks at night are more like churches than churches are. If so, we half expected St. Peter to take our ticket stubs.

We ate some chicken fingers and French fries, took our soft drinks and made our way to the seats to watch batting practice. Bonds hit several out and it was fun, but the thing that amazed me was watching Clemens warm up. He was throwing balls with Jorge Posada in centerfield. In a few moments, he and his catch buddy had over half the outfield between them and Clemens was firing strikes from left center all the way to right field. My arm hurt just watching.

But it was hot that day. We kept drinks coming and programs spread on our legs to protect us from the sun. Finally the game started. It was a great game. Clemens pitched a good game and the battle with Bonds was amazing. He did not give Bonds anything to hit. Finally, in the fifth inning or so, Clemens came in tight. Bonds backed out and took off his elbow pad daring Clemens to come in there again. Clemens had hit him once already. It was classic baseball. Bonds went 0 for 1 with a pair of walks. In the end, Nick Johnson doubled off the wall late in the game and the Yankees won 4-2.

The subway ride back revealed that Patrick loved the train. It was a fun experience, but I think it was for two reasons: one, it was much cooler, and two it was on the ground. We got off at West 79th Street and walked the half block to our hotel and cooled off.

We were in the Promised Land and had paid homage to the temple of baseball. All we needed was a good supper, a cool room, and some sleep. Then we would do it all again the next day.

On 10 June we woke up and went to the Jackson Hole for breakfast. The Jackson Hole was like the perfect eatery for Patrick and me. One of the best hamburgers I ever had and in the morning some of the best pancakes ever flipped. After eating far too much, we lumbered back to the hotel to get ready for the best day of the trip. At 10:00 A.M. we went to the Museum of Natural History. Patrick loves natural history and this was his turf. He knew enough to give a tour in the place. While the dinosaur bones are impressive, there was not a boring moment in the entire museum. On top of that, the Baseball Hall of Fame exhibit was there, too.

About halfway through, our camera showed we were out of film. We had taken a lot of pictures at the game the day before, and had taken a lot at the museum. I sat down and discovered there was *no* film in the camera. All the pictures we took at Yankee stadium existed only in our memories. We raced back to the start of the museum and retook the pictures there. We laughed but there were so many photos we lost from the previous day that I nearly cried. Thankfully, we were going to another game that night so we could take some more.

That afternoon we got on the subway and arrived earlier to the stadium than we had on the day before. This time, we bought a hotdog and drink each and paid a total of $6.00.

We visited the souvenir shops. Patrick was wearing his Diamondbacks hat and t-shirt. I was wearing my Yankees hat. Wearing Diamondbacks stuff at Yankee stadium was a bit like a Philistine visiting Solomon's temple.

Our seats were on the second row, in the upper deck, behind home plate. Since it was a night game, and the sun was not in our eyes, they were the best seats we could imagine. As the sun began to go behind the clouds, the heat let up and the night air cooled us. The sellout crowd was like a family gathering at a holiday feast with one purpose and in one accord. The game was omnipresent, and it was perfect.

It was better than church. Jim Dant, my pastor at Highland Hills Baptist Church, once preached a sermon on how the Waffle House is a bit like church. That night in Yankee Stadium I felt as if time had stopped and everything was somehow going to be okay. If my first game at Yankee Stadium had been special, this one was equal. Though Patrick nearly ate my wallet empty, I was happy; he was happy. I wished that Susan and David could have been there, but I knew she would understand. David would not. I know what his response would be: "When I get older like John Patrick will you take me?"

The game. Randy Johnson pitched for the Diamondbacks. Derek Jeter homered, but the Diamondbacks had the lead until the bottom on the eighth when Shane Spencer hit a grand slam. The crowd erupted. In part because of the game itself, but in part because of the game seven loss to the Diamondbacks nearly eight months earlier. Patrick was standing and screaming against the 60,000 that cheered Spencer. The Yankees won 7-5. Patrick was disappointed with the outcome, but the atmosphere and the game were memorable and electric. Patrick has hated the Yankees ever since.

On the subway back to the hotel, the train was packed. Several adults consoled Patrick when they saw him wearing his hat and shirt. It was one of the kindest things I ever saw. The stereotypical New York Yankee fan was nowhere to be found. These were good people. They were not obnoxious and rude as portrayed in Hollywood or by Bosox fans.

Patrick at the Yankee Stadium subway stop.

The next day we went to midtown Manhattan and spent the day at FAO Schwarz and Borders and eating hotdogs and exploring the city. Then, the next day, we went home.

Our pilgrimage was over. Yet, like any pilgrimage, you never go home the same. We were both changed. We had the time of our lives. Our journey led us to a deeper appreciation of each other. We bonded out of love and necessity. Having never been there before, Patrick was the only person I knew there. I felt more like a father on that trip than I had ever felt before.

One moment that is more memorable than most others was Patrick reading a Redwall book in front of Yankee Stadium. That moment put it all in perspective. Not being a big baseball fan, Patrick was saying to me that I can take him to a ball game, but he was going to be himself. He loves to read, and his singular act was an act of independence. Yet, I have read to him since he was born; he has always been surrounded by books, but I never oppressed him with baseball.

And then there was the smile I saw on his face as we walked through the Museum of Natural History, or while we were in the bookstore on Broadway, or eating a hotdog on the street. His smile was the world to me.

Patrick and New York changed me. We had traveled to the Promised Land of baseball. It was full of life and it filled us with excitement and brought us to one final conclusion: we wanted to go home. Susan and David were there and that is where we belonged.

The plane ride home was long. The shuttle was even longer. But when we finally saw Susan and David, we realized that the real Promised Land was wherever the four of us were together. I told Susan and David that we were elated to be safe at home. She asked if I would ever want to go back. Thinking about being in the great temple, I smiled and said, "How about next week, but all of us this time."

I found my "calling." Looking back at that moment I saw Susan and David I now know that I was called to be the best husband and father I could be. I did not recognize it then. I recognize it now in writing this story. It was a moment when it became clear what I was to do, but I was not paying attention. We do not always recognize the moments when they occur. Often, it is in the act of remembering that we realize it. The "calling" in my life has been redefined many times at many moments. I had been so concerned with finding that call that I had often missed it. I was too busy looking when I should have been listening, talking when I should have been praying, working when I should have been playing, crying when I should have been laughing.

My calling had been the same since my first week of seminary, but only recently made sense. Dr.

Page Kelley was teaching Amos and on the first day of my first class, he was talking about Amos's vies of justice and he pointed us to the prophet Micah referring to what God requires of us:

—Do justice,
—love kindness (*hesed*=unconditional love),
—and to walk humbly with God.
    (Micah 6:8b)

This is all I needed to remember, and when I saw them, that is what I thought about. Was I reinterpreting? Perhaps.

I don't think Patrick will ever forget that trip. And I hope David will go with me sometime. But, most of all, I wish my dad could have gone. At the time, he was in a nursing home. He and I often talked about wanting to go together. I told him that I had taken Patrick to Yankee Stadium and he mustered a smile and whispered, "You did!" I never wanted anything as much in life than to have gone to Yankee Stadium with my dad. But, in a way, we did go there. Being there without him but thinking of him was an amazing feeling. He had been to a game there when he served in the National Guard in New York. And now I had been. We were there together, united in our hopes and dreams.

He died seven months later.

10

Field of Dreams

> I count the loves of my life: Annie, Karin, Iowa, Baseball. The great god baseball.
> —W. P. Kinsella, *Shoeless Joe*

> Today you will be with me in Paradise.
> —Luke 23:43

The film *Field of Dreams* is astonishing. People either love it or hate it. It's either understood by those who love it or scoffed at by those who don't. With its fantasy elements and far-reaching plot to its portrayal of a wife who is understanding beyond belief, or from its odd use of time travel to its setting in an Iowa cornfield, this movie evokes strong reactions. Most baseball fans love the film. They "understand" what is going on. Some people, like my wife Susan, love the film not because they understand the baseball parts of the film necessarily, but because it is a romantic view of family life and is a happy story.

The film is astonishing because it captures so much of the wonder of the book on which it is based, *Shoeless Joe* by W. P. Kinsella. The book began as a short story, "Shoeless Joe Comes to Iowa." Later Kinsella developed it into a full-length novel, *Shoeless Joe*. The book is about a man named Ray Kinsella who, along with his wife and daughter, live on a farm in Iowa. As a baseball-loving farmer, Ray begins hearing voices and soon begins building the left field portion of a baseball park. He thinks he has built it for Shoeless Joe Jackson. Shoeless Joe was a member of the 1919 Chicago White ("Black") Sox, the favorite to win the World Series, but they mysteriously lost to the Cincinnati Reds. After they lost, a scandal broke loose and it was determined that eight of the White Sox players took money to throw the series to the Reds. All eight were kicked out of baseball and to this day diehard fans are still trying to get Shoeless Joe into the hall of fame because although he received money to throw the series, there is no proof by his performance that he actually did.

Also in this fantasy of a book, Ray kidnaps J. D. Salinger and brings him back to this yet-unfinished ballpark. They meet Archie "Moonlight" Graham as a young man just starting out in baseball, although in real time Graham had been dead for several years (that time-travel thing). Things not in the movie: Throw in Ray's twin and that his twin is in the circus and that Ray gets his gun and tries to defend his family against his wife's brother, and then throw in a man from a retirement home who claims to be the oldest living Chicago Cub and finally the completion of the ballpark and so forth, and you have a wonderful book. Obviously, there are some fundamental differences between the movie and the book. Most telling, in the book, Ray and his twin have a walk and talk with their dad, and the movie ends differently from the book.

While the book is a great read and worthy of several readings, the movie is also worth several viewings. In fact, it is on some TV channel or other every March just before baseball season begins.

In the film, Ray Kinsella hears voices telling him "If you build it, he will come"; "Ease his pain;" and "Go the distance." Is this God's voice? No. The voice's identity is left for the audience to ponder. Near the end, just when one thinks it is the voice of Shoeless Joe Jackson, we discover not only who the voice belongs to, but to whom it was referring the entire time. It is Ray's voice speaking to himself. The "he" is not Shoeless Joe, but Ray's father, who had died years earlier.

The film ends with Ray playing catch with his dad, who has shown up to play catcher for the team facing the White Sox. Ray introduces his father to his wife and to his daughter. Then Ray and his dad have a game of catch. As the camera pulls back, one can see the line of traffic that is forming to come and see baseball in this cornfield baseball stadium. While it may sound corny (no pun intended), the ending was perfect. There is nothing better and more like home for a boy than playing catch with his dad.

In 1991, while I was teaching at Simmons University in Louisville, Kentucky, Ms. Bradley from the office interrupted me in the middle of a class. My father had had a stroke. I dismissed class, went home where Susan had almost finished packing, put Patrick in the car seat, and took off on our six-hour trek home to Cleveland, Tennessee. Dad had had a mini-stroke and would be all right eventually, but at the same time the warning was that these kinds of strokes could keep coming unless he quit smoking and drinking and started exercising.

He tried to exercise but it never caught hold of him. He tried walking but unless he quit the two vices in his life, then his attempts at walking were nearly futile. After a few more occurrences, his health began to deteriorate and he slowly lost the ability to walk or drive. In late 2000, he was put into a nursing home facility by my mom and my brother Mike in what has to be one of the most courageous and difficult things they have ever done. Mom could no longer take care of him. He required constant supervision and she could not, no matter how much she wanted to and how much she loved him.

For two years he lived in a home not his own, all the time with the hope that he might return to his own house and his own bed. As much as he and my mom wanted that, it would never happen.

In December 2002, he took a sharp turn for the worse. Susan, Patrick, David, and I made four trips to Cleveland that winter. During the third trip Mike and I took turns staying with dad at night. I would stay until around 3 or 4 in the morning and Mike would relieve me. We did this for two nights before Susan and I returned to Macon. On the second night I actually thought he was doing better. I could barely understand anything he said, however. Sometimes he would lie there and have pain on his face. Sometimes he looked hungry. But mostly, he looked tired.

I tried to tell him all the things I could remember that he and I used to do. I spoke of how he taught me to love the Yankees and Braves and everything baseball. I spoke of how we use to play catch and go to baseball games. But we also went to football and basketball games. I spoke of the time when he taught me to drive and when I had my first wreck. As a father myself, I now understand that he was not so much upset at me about the wreck as he was both scared of my near death and relieved that I was okay.

I spoke to him about many things that night. But

I most of all remember holding him and trying to help him relax so he could rest. Just when I thought he was asleep, he opened his eyes and asked me, "You wanna pass a baseball?"

I nodded, and in my mind I thought, "More than anything."

Finally, on 5 January 2003 he died. It was Susan's birthday—a Sunday afternoon—when mom called to tell me that he had passed.

We packed up the van and made the trip to Cleveland. We did the funeral home visitation and saw lots of people we had not seen much of in a long time, and now we saw them for the wrong reasons.

The next day was the funeral. My brothers and my mother asked me to "preach" the funeral. I had buried my father's parents. And now I would bury him. I have never been as honored to do anything in my life. At the same time, I have never been as emotionally drained of anything in my life, either. Tom also said a few words that day. Mike spoke too, but he spoke in silence. He is, in many ways, the son most like our father.

After the funeral, we drove to the graveside and had a brief service there. Following those brief minutes, we all departed. We went back to mom's house where many people came and ate lunch with us and we talked and talked. Soon we left. Susan and the boys and I left for Macon. Mom needed time to herself and so did the rest of us.

That afternoon, they laid my dad in the ground. He now resided in a field of dreams. He was safe at home.

That night, back home in Macon, Georgia, we went to bed exhausted over the day and the past month. In the middle of the night, I sat upright and all I could think of was that my dad was in the cold, hard ground. Soon, I lay back down. I tried to think about the happy times and I settled on playing catch with him in the backyard. I was crying and I missed him. But I kept thinking about the two of us passing baseball. Those were special moments. They were moments that are still as fresh in my memory as seeing Yankee Stadium, as seeing Roger Clemens, Barry Bonds, Randy Johnson, Derek Jeter, and Shane Spencer. Soon I fell asleep.

That next spring was difficult. I never expected the residual feelings from his death. At times I felt abandoned and at other times I felt totally alone in the world. Baseball season was set to open, and I think USA was going to air *Field of Dreams* on the weekend before the season opener. I had seen that movie at least once every year since it came out, but there was no way I could watch it again. Not this year.

A year later, during January 2003, *Field of Dreams* was showing on two consecutive nights on the same network. The first night I watched most of it with my son David. But we missed the last thirty minutes. That was okay, because I was not sure I could see that part yet.

On the following night I turned on the TV and I saw, almost by accident—or was it?—the last twenty minutes of *Field of Dreams*. I only cried a couple of tears, but David was there with me once again. I asked him if he would play baseball with me when it got warmer outside. He said, "Sure."

David takes a swing "[o]ne day that spring...."

One day that spring, Patrick and I played catch. In between throws, I threw a whiffle ball for David to hit. I was playing baseball with my sons in my own backyard. As we played, the trees swayed in the March winds. There was no voice telling me to build anything, or telling me to go the distance, or to go and teach, but there was the calmness and excitement that comes with spring, and the sound of the bat on the ball, even if it was a plastic bat. Susan was looking out the window, smiling. It may have been a backyard, but it was, for that afternoon, a field of dreams.

I count the three loves of my life: God, family, and baseball.

11

Recreation[3]

> Well, beat the drum and hold the phone—
> the sun came out today!
> We're born again, there's new grass on the field...
> —John C. Fogerty

> From those holiest waters I returned to her reborn, a
> tree renewed, in bloom with newborn foliage,
> immaculate, eager to rise, now ready for the stars.
> —Dante, *Purgatorio*, 33:142–45 (Musa)

After my father's death, I had a very hard time adjusting to mortality. I knew all the right things to think and say thanks to my seminary training. But the real experience is a far better, more brutal teacher than

---

[3] As in *re-creation*, an act of renewal.

you can learn from any books. Between January and April, I had many moments of tremendous sadness and melancholy. I knew I needed help, but I was new at this and thought of turning to my pastor, visiting my mother, or taking the family on a weekend vacation. Soon, I realized that I needed to have some time to myself. Alone. I needed to be *re*-created.

I needed to get away, and thanks to SkyMiles, I had a free plane ticket anywhere in the US. I also had an understanding wife who not only did not mind my going but she even encouraged it.

I flew to New York City and was by myself in the greatest city on the planet. I was alone in the midst of millions of people. That's just where I needed to be.

I went to see *La Traviata* at the Metropolitan Opera. I saw Anne-Sophie Mutter perform Andre Previn's *Violin Concerto*. I saw the Picasso-Matisse exhibit at the Museum of Modern Art in Queens, of all places (the city site was under renovation). I saw *Chicago* on Broadway. I went to bookstores, went by the American Bible Society, and the New York Public Library. I was doing something every moment.

George Steiner says that God is found in acts of creation. While some would say that music, opera, drama, and literature are only cultural forms, I agree with Steiner. I felt closer to God at Lincoln Center than I have ever felt in a church. When Anne-Sophie Mutter began playing I felt as if I had been lifted to the clouds where angels watched in reverential silence. It reminded me of my first visit to Yankee Stadium, only there was an important difference. While you watch a game and you watch all the people at the stadium, at a concert like this you are forced to watch yourself. Your attention is inward.

Similarly, I believed in God's creative powers more than ever when I saw the works of Picasso, Matisse, Pollock, and Van Gogh's *Starry Night*. While there I was being recreated.

But one thing I did not do. I did not go to a Yankees game. They were out of town. If God is to be found in acts of creation, then the opera, the concert, the art exhibition, and even the literature was God's way to recreate me anew. I could not go to a game. Not even a Mets game. I don't think I could have survived watching a game. I thought all I needed was this trip. While it was a great time, healing is rarely a pretty thing. Attending concerts, plays, movies, and visiting great sites was a means to an end. But one thing remained, and it was the most important.

The night before I left, I talked to Susan on the phone. She was very concerned about me. Her voice on the phone was one mixed with absolute love and certain fear. She was afraid something might happen to me. After I hung up, I felt alone. I was struck with the horrific thought that I might never see her and my sons again. I slept very little that night—if any, it was out of pure exhaustion. It was time to go home.

My plane ride home was good but not fast enough, and the shuttle ride to Macon was long. I drove my car from the shuttle service to my house, smiling all the way.

When I walked into my home, into the arms of my family, my life was different. God had wiped away my tears. All things were made new. God was more present in my family at that moment than he was at any other moment in my life. Indeed, as Buechner said, life is grace. Just as the love of family helped William Styron to overcome his depression—and me of my melancholia seven years earlier—my love for my family and their love for me recreated me.

And I can still see the stars.

Appendix

Books on Baseball, Family, and God

> It's designed to break your heart. The game begins in the spring, when everything is new again, and it blossoms in the summer, filling the afternoons and evenings, and then as soon as the chill rain comes, it stops, and leaves you to face the fall alone.
> —A. Bartlett Giamatti

> Study to show thyself approved...
> —2 Timothy 2:15

The books on the interconnection of baseball, family, and God are few. But some books have had an impact on my thinking and my experience. While there is a large number of baseball players who have been religious, these are some that I am familiar with and whose stories of faith and baseball have been inspirational.

Baseball and religion have always been a part of each other. Whether it is W. P. Kinsella or Annie Savoy, religious language is often the only adequate language to describe baseball. Some believe that baseball is a civil religion, and I would agree. But what one sees today is too much. When a player trots home and points to heaven what it seems to me they are saying is that God helped them hit that home run at that time. If that is true, then the basic problem is that why would God help any player against another team? God doesn't care who wins or plays well in baseball. God cares about people loving people. Players like Sandy Koufax, Christy Mathewson, Lou Gehrig, Jackie Robinson, Hank Greenberg, and countless others never went around pointing to heaven and wearing a 3-pound gold cross on their chest. They played because they loved the game. But it was never more than God. Baseball was never their God, although it may have been close.

Hank Aaron

Aaron, Hank with Lonnie Wheeler. *I Had a Hammer: The Hank Aaron Story*. New York: HarperCollins, 1991.

Stanton, Tom. *Hank Aaron and the Homerun that Changed America*. New York: Wm. Morrow, 2004.

As chapter 4 above indicates, Hank Aaron was a childhood favorite. There has yet to be a major biography written about Aaron. It will come soon. I just hope that it is worthy of the subject. Until then, one should read and reread his autobiography, *I Had a Hammer*. I still remember the day boss and friend Chris Conver saw the announcement of this book in a Harper catalog at the bookstore where we worked. It is not a religious autobiography, but Hank did something before other African-American baseball players at the major league level: he was the star on the first major league team in the South, and that was 1966. While all of America had great racial tensions during the 1940s–1960s, to have been in Atlanta in the 1960s was a trial by fire. Stories of Jackie Robinson are well known, but more should be talked about Aaron and what he lived through in Atlanta. Not only did he live through it, he excelled as a major leaguer in the midst of hatred that would make Satan blush. "What if" questions usually irritate me, but what Aaron's stats looked like if he had played in today's more relaxed (although not perfect) climate rather than in the 1960s has always intrigued me. He was a brave man, and was a great baseball player.

Lou Gehrig

Eig, Jonathan. *Luckiest Man: The Life and Death of Lou Gehrig*. New York: Simon & Schuster, 2005.

Luce, Willard and Celia. *Lou Gehrig: Iron Man of*

Baseball. Champaign IL: Garrard Publishing Company, 1970.

Robinson, Ray. *Iron Horse: Lou Gehrig in His Time*. New York: Norton, 1990.

When I was a kid, I read a book (by Willard and Celia Luce) about Lou Gehrig that had a tremendous impact on my baseball experience. I read all about his family and his childhood and his great career in the shadow of Babe Ruth. His graceful approach towards people and his unbelievable work ethic influenced me greatly. But it was the way he died that affected me the most, as it has so many others. Gehrig has been idolized in baseball lore. The book by Robinson and the newer one by Eigs give a much more accurate portrait of Gehrig. He still deserves to be remembered.

Hank Greenberg

Greenberg, Hank, and Ira Berkow. *Hank Greenberg: The Story of My Life*. Benhmark Press, 2001.

The Life and Times of Hank Greenberg. DVD. Twentieth Century Fox, 2003.

If Hank Greenberg had not been Jewish, he would probably be remembered as one of the greatest players ever. He was and he is. The DVD mentioned above is spectacular.

Sandy Koufax

Leavy, Jane. *Sandy Koufax: A Lefty's Legacy*. New York: HarperCollins, 2002.

When Sandy Koufax decided to sit out the first game of the 1965 World Series because it was to be played on Yom Kippur (the Jewish Day of Atonement) he made an explicitly religious statement: his Jewish faith was more important than baseball. *Sports Illustrated* named him its favorite athlete of the twentieth century and said he had the left arm of God. In the Hebrew Bible (the Christian Old Testament), the right arm of God was all-powerful. As a Hebrew student I had wondered what God had used the left arm for.

Koufax was an amazing pitcher. The fact that his religious faith was more important than baseball is not often talked about in our secular world. Like Christy Mathewson decades before, Koufax put God first. Of course, Mathewson was a Christian, but he and Koufax had two things in common: baseball and God.

Christy Mathewson

Deford, Frank. *The Old Ballgame: How John McGraw, Christy Mathewson, and the New York Giants*

Created Modern Baseball. New York: Atlantic Monthly Press, 2005.

Greenberg, Eric Rolfe. *The Celebrant: A Novel.* Lincoln: University of Nebraska Press, 1993 [reprint].

Robinson, Ray. *Matty: An American Hero: Christy Mathewson of the New York Giants.* New York: Oxford University Press, 1994.

Seib, Philip. *The Player: Christy Mathewson, Baseball, and the American Century.* New York: Four Walls, Eight Windows, 2003.

I love reading about baseball of decades past. When I first read about Christy Mathewson, I thought his story was too manufactured to be true: no one is that respectable. But he was. Each of the books above is unique, and all should be read by anyone interested in how a Christian can play major league baseball and keep his integrity. Anyone who promises his mother that he would never pitch on a Sunday and keeps the promise deserves to be read about.

Jackie Robinson

Rampersad, Arnold. *Jackie Robinson: A Biography.* New York: Knopf, 1997. (Paperback, Ballentine, 1998.)

Robinson, Jackie. *"I Never Had It Made."* New York: Putnam, 1972. (Paperback, Ecco, 2003.)

Too much has been written on Jackie Robinson. Because of this flood of material, his accomplishments are often watered down in legend rather than the brutal truth of his experience. For the best book on Robinson, turn to Arnold Rampersad's biography that shows how turbulent and amazing Robinson's life was. He would never have made it had it not been for his faith and his family. It should not be forgotten that Robinson was a great player on a team that originally despised him, not to mention a league and a country that prayed that he would fail. Strength and courage like his are of a unique source. He would be quick to acknowledge that without God, his life was nothing.

Other Books

The literature on baseball, family, and God is scarce. The writing on religion and baseball is not much more than that. There are a few books that need to be mentioned.

Allen E. Hye's *The Great God Baseball: Religion in Modern Baseball Fiction* (Macon: Mercer University Press, 2004) looks at religious themes in baseball fiction. The novels discussed there could double the size of this list. The novels themselves are special because it is in baseball novels that one can see the interconnection of baseball, family, and religion most vividly. Hye will make you want to read all nine books, and that is the mark of a well-written book of literary criticism.

Joseph L. Price's edited collection *From Season to Season: Sports as American Religion* (Macon: Mercer University Press, 2001 [2005, paperback]) has three great essays on baseball and religion. Price's own essay "The Pitcher's Mound as Cosmic Mountain: The Religious Significance of Baseball" is a penetrating contribution to the understanding of baseball as religion. Paul C. Johnson's "The Fetish and McGwire's Balls" must be read to be believed. And Peter Williams's "Every Religion Needs a Martyr: The Role of Matty, Gehrig, and Clemente in the National Faith" is a must-read. Joe has a new book coming out in the spring of 2006 on baseball and religion that will also astound.

Christopher H. Evans's and William R. Herzog's *The Faith of 50 Million: Baseball, Religion, and American Culture* (Louisville: Westminster/JohnKnox, 2002) is a solid collection of essays on baseball and religion. Written by religion scholars, this book is the best book available on the connection of baseball and religion in America.

Finally, Dave Dravecky's *Called Up: Stories of Life and Faith from the Great Game of Baseball* is a must-read. It's full of stories and all-star teams and Yogisms and all kinds of things that amuse and inspire. It is a bit forced at times. Dravecky recalls a great story that seems to have very little to do with religion and then he offers a Christian principle to apply it but the book is worth the time. One thing is for sure, that Dravecky himself is a testament to the life of faith.